Contents

KW-480-445

Introduction   5

MODULE 1   **The Apostrophe** 9
Unit 1   Introduction   9
         Belonging   10
Unit 2   Using the Apostrophe with Words ending in -s   13
Unit 3   Using the Apostrophe when Letters are missed out   15

MODULE 2   **The Sentence, or Period: Space: Capital** 18
Unit 1   Capital Letters and Full Stops   19
Unit 2   Layout   21
Unit 3   Comma Splice   24
         Capital Letters   26
         Supplementary Exercises   28

MODULE 3   **Spelling One** 29
Unit 1   Introduction   29
         Vowel Clusters *ie* and *ei*   31
Unit 2   Consonant Clusters *ch, tch, ck*   35
Unit 3   Word Endings *-ary, -ery*   38

MODULE 4   **Spelling Two** 42
Unit 1   Adding Endings   42
Unit 2   Vowel Cluster *ea*   45
         Consonant Clusters *cc, wh, th*   46
Unit 3   Word Ending *-y*   49

MODULE 5   **Spelling Three** 53
Unit 1   Word Ending silent *-e*   53
Unit 2   Vowel Cluster *ui*   54
         Consonant Clusters *sc, ss, mm, mb*   55
Unit 3   Word Endings *-ful, -ly, -ment, -tion*   60

MODULE 6   **Spelling Four** 64
Unit 1   Vowel Cluster *ou* 64
Unit 2   Vowel Cluster *au* 69
           Consonant Clusters *ght, kn* 71
Unit 3   Word Endings *-ance, -ence, -able, -ible* 73

MODULE 7   **The Comma** 77
Unit 1   Items in a List 77
Unit 2   Commas used to mark off Parts of a Sentence 80
Unit 3   Joining Sentences 83
           Supplementary Exercises 86

MODULE 8   **The Paragraph** 88
Unit 1   Introduction 88
           Why have Paragraphs? 90
           Planning Paragraphs 94
           Setting Out Paragraphs 97
Unit 2   Letter Writing: Introduction 100
           Business Letters 100
           Job Applications 105
           Supplementary Exercises 108
Unit 3   Personal Letters 109
           Letter Writing: Paragraphs 111
           Longer Letters 114

MODULE 9   **Direct Speech** 117
Unit 1   Introduction 117
           Speaker: Speech 120
Unit 2   Speech: Speaker 125
Unit 3   Speech: Speaker: Speech 128

Answers 131

Spelling List 156

Introduction

It may be said that there are broadly three levels of skill required in writing. At the lowest level there are the 'clerical skills' of writing: this includes the ability to punctuate your message so that it is understood by the reader; and the ability to spell at least the commonest words in the language. A higher level of skill is involved in handling the complexities of grammar, the higher management and control of language. The highest level of skill in writing is demonstrated in the ability to handle tone, to select vocabulary with sensitivity and imagination, to achieve elegance as well as clarity; these matters are covered by the concept of style.

We must say right away that this book deals only with the first and lowest level of writing skills, the clerical skills of language. We chose to do this because, in spite of the apparently modest level of the aim, we consider that this particular set of skills underlies all other writing skills. No matter how high or fine the writer's style, he or she has to take account of the conventions of punctuation and the spelling system. But more important to us was our awareness that it is often at this level of skill in writing that most of our students and future adults are judged to fail. When employers and others complain that standards have fallen, it is usually about performance in punctuation and spelling that they are talking. If we could improve our teaching of these simple skills, we would give our students greater confidence in writing and, perhaps, increase their ability to benefit from instruction in the higher order skills of language.

It was partly with a view to providing the teacher with more class time to devote to the creative purpose of teaching the higher order skills that we devised the system of assessment and follow-up instruction in the mechanical skills of writing upon which this book is based. We have long felt that traditional class teaching of punctuation and spelling is wasteful, both of the teacher's time and that of a majority of the students. In most classes, but particularly in mixed-ability classes such as are commonly found at Primary and at the early stages of Secondary school, during any lesson on, say, the comma, there will be those who don't need the lesson and those, perhaps a sizeable number, who may well need the lesson but who, for one reason or another, are not ready for it. In circumstances like these we can but hope that the ones who both need the lesson and are ready to take it in are all present and fully attentive on the day the lesson is given! In spelling, as many teachers know, students' problems tend to be highly specific and are not in general very successfully dealt with through the medium of class instruction. It is not much use giving a particular student lessons on the 'ei/ie' distinction when his problem is that he cannot turn 'y' singulars into plurals!

The basic strategy which this book is advocating, therefore, is:
a) To diagnose each student's weaknesses in the range of mechanical skills which are outlined in the specimen assessment form shown below;
b) Following this assessment, to direct each student to a particular programme of study, in this book called a Module, which is designed to help them acquire the competence which they lack.

Making the Assessment

It is very important that any form of diagnostic assessment which is being suggested for teaching should be simple and quick to operate. It must not involve a lot of form-filling, yet it must provide a valid record of the pupil's progress. Here is a specimen of the assessment form which we advocate for this purpose and which we call a *Basic Writing Skills Identifier*.

BASIC WRITING SKILLS IDENTIFIER								
NAME						CLASS		SESSION
DATE:	PERIOD: SPACE: CAPITAL	COMMA	APOSTROPHE	DIRECT SPEECH	PARAGRAPHING	SPELLING	COMMENTS	FOLLOW-UP

BASIS

An Individualised Approach
to Basic Writing Skills

Pat McLaughlin
and Ken MacAskill

OLIVER & BOYD

Acknowledgments

The authors and publishers thank the following for permission to use extracts from the undernoted books:

William Collins Sons & Co Ltd for *The Master of Morgana* by Allan Campbell McLean, Curtis Brown Ltd for *The Treasure of the Sierra Madre* by B. Traven and Penguin Books Ltd for *Smith* by Leon Garfield.

Oliver & Boyd
Robert Stevenson House
1–3 Baxter's Place
Leith Walk
Edinburgh EH1 3BB

A Division of Longman Group Limited

First published 1980
Second impression 1982

ISBN 0 05 003252 6

Phototypeset in V.I.P. Palatino by
Western Printing Services Ltd, Bristol
Printed in Hong Kong by
Wilture Enterprises (International) Ltd

It is a simple matter to run off copies of a form based on this model for each student who is included in the assessment programme.

The assessment upon which this system is based is carried out in each class four times a year. As a result of tests conducted over a period of years and in a large number of schools, we have found that one hundred and fifty words of a student's continuous prose are ideal for the purpose. This piece of writing need not be done specially for the occasion. It need not even come from work done in the English classroom. Within a policy for language across the curriculum it is perfectly appropriate to assess a student's written work in any other specialist subject. This sample of writing is corrected, the errors in spelling and punctuation are counted and the resulting scores recorded in the Identifier. This provides a profile of the student's ability in the basic level of writing skill.

Where there is one error or less in any component the figure 1 is recorded in the appropriate column. This indicates that the student's ability in this particular sub-skill is *satisfactory* and needn't lead to any follow-up work at this stage. If there are *two* or *three* errors, then the number 2 is inserted. This score indicates that the student's command of this sub-skill is less than satisfactory and therefore *requires attention*. This would normally lead to the study of the appropriate modules. If there are more than three errors, this is classified as *weak* and the number 3 is inserted in the Identifier at the appropriate place. This classification would almost always lead to follow-up work.

It is our experience that in all classes using this method you do get, in fact, genuine profiles. Very seldom do you find students in any class with a complete string of either ones or threes. This is partly explained by the fact that this form of assessment does not attempt to discriminate between one student and another in terms of natural ability. It is a strength of the system that it treats every student as a special case who, at his own level of ability, has specific learning problems. For this reason it is vital that the scripts used for the assessment should always accompany the Identifier since without them it is meaningless. As these scripts are assembled in each student's portfolio, the pattern of an individual student's difficulties will begin to emerge.

The follow-up study
The core of this book contains the series of modules corresponding to the sub-skills classified in the Identifier. After the assessment has been made, the teacher and the student agree on the particular module which is to be studied. At the times set aside for the class work on these

modules, the students go to the chosen part of the book and begin to work their way through the material. For the most part the modules are self-directing and so the calls upon the teacher during these times should be reduced, allowing him or her to adopt more fully the role of consultant. It is usually found that a self-pacing programme of work like this is very much to the taste of the students. At the same time it is recognised that the teacher is the single most valuable resource in any classroom and so at specific points in each of the programmes the student is asked to show particular pieces of work to the teacher and thus a degree of student-teacher contact is guaranteed.

Each module is divided up into units, of which there are normally three per module. Where it has proved possible, we have incorporated pre-tests into the modules. If the student passes one of these unit tests without error, he or she may omit the unit which the test covers and move on to the next one. In this way the students discover the exact point at which their difficulties occur and do not have to waste time doing work which has been mastered.

Needless to say, if there are any students in the class who have no problems in any aspect of these skills, then they should be assigned alternative work when the other members of the class are engaged on module work.

MODULE 1

The Apostrophe

Unit 1

INTRODUCTION

Here is an example of the apostrophe
John's pal came to the door.

Here is another example
The footballers' cars were in the car-park.

Here are some more examples
I'm going.
We'll see you later.
My sister's out.
You'd better go.

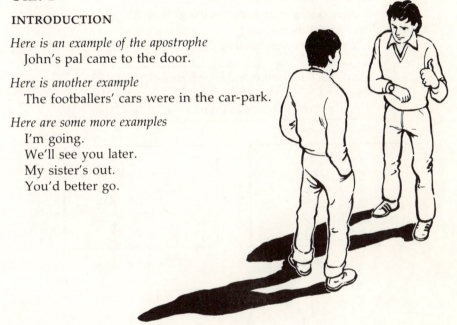

As you can see, the *apostrophe* is a mark like a comma which hangs *just above* the letters of a word.

   e.g. sister's

Sometimes, the *apostrophe* comes *in between* the letters of a word.

   e.g. John's   I'm

Sometimes, it comes at the *end of a word.*

   e.g. footballers'

There are only *two* uses of the *apostrophe.*

1. To show that something *belongs* to someone or something. We will call this *Belonging* (Units 1 and 2).
2. To show that one or more letters have been missed out (Unit 3).

Belonging

Unit Test

Write out the following sentences, putting in the apostrophes.

1. My mothers sisters are coming today.
2. The horses neck was glistening with sweat.
3. He kicked his opponents ankle.
4. The teachers books were lying on the girls desk.
5. What is the doctors number?
6. The childrens cries were not heard.

Now check with the answers on page 131.
If you made no mistakes go to Unit 2 on page 13.
If you made any mistakes continue with this unit.

This is Joe.

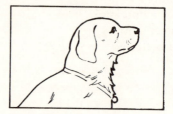

This is *his* dog.

This is the dog that *belongs* to Joe.

Another way of saying the same thing is:

This is *Joe's* dog.

By using the *apostrophe* plus *s*, you have written a neater sentence and *saved yourself four words.*

This is the dog that belongs to Joe. *(8 words)*
This is Joe's dog.   *(4 words)*

If you did not know how to use the *apostrophe* you would be a very clumsy writer.

EXERCISE 1:

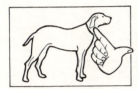
The hand is pointing at the dog's ear.

Write out in your exercise book in a full sentence just like the one above which part of the dog is being pointed at in the pictures.

Check with the answers on page 131.

EXERCISE 2

Write out the following sentences in your exercise book, putting in the apostrophe where it has been missed out.

1. Joes dog is called Toby.
2. Joes family are very fond of Toby.
3. The postman, however, is not very keen on Joes dog.

4. One day Toby took a bite out of the postmans trousers.
5. The postman complained to the police about the dogs behaviour.
6. A policeman called at Joes house to talk about the dogs attack on the postman.
7. Joes mother invited the policeman into the house and asked him to sit in the familys best chair.
8. Toby was nobodys fool. He knew the difference between a policeman and a postman. He sat looking up at the policemans face and wagged his tail.
9. After drinking the tea which Joes mother made for him, the policeman patted Toby's head and said he seemed a very friendly little dog. In return, Toby licked the policemans hand.
10. The policeman went away saying that he was sure it was all the postmans fault.

Show your completed sentences to your teacher.

EXERCISE 3

Write out the following list in your exercise book, as shown below, filling in the blanks by using the apostrophe *plus* s.

This is what you should write

Without the apostrophe
The pages of the book

Using the apostrophe
The book's pages

Without the apostrophe

1. The leaves of the tree
2. The spout of the kettle
3. The whistle of the train
4. The trousers which the boy was wearing
5. The bottom of the ship
6. The boy who works for the butcher
7. The visit made by the doctor
8. The smile of the chorus-girl

9. The glow of the sun
10. The gloves of the boxer
11. The verdict reached by the jury
12. The passport which belonged to the American
13. The ribbon of the typewriter
14. The trigger of the rifle
15. The knock of the postman

Now check with the answers on page 131.

Unit 2 Using the apostrophe with words ending in -s

Unit Test

*Write out the following sentences in your exercise book putting in
the apostrophes.*

1. The monkeys paws were wet. (There are two monkeys.)
2. The cars axles were covered in dust. (There are three cars.)
3. The cricketers coats lay on the ground. (There are eleven cricketers.)
4. The soldiers rifles lay in a heap (It is a regiment of soldiers.)
5. The twins faces were exactly alike.
6. The childrens presents were under the Christmas tree.

> *Now check with the answers on page 132.*
> *If you made no mistakes, go to Unit 3 on page 15.*
> *If you made any mistakes continue with this unit.*

If you were asked to rewrite the phrase *the wheels of the car* using the
apostrophe, you would be able to do it easily. It is, of course, *the car's
wheels*.
But what if there were *two* cars – the wheels of the *cars*?
Well, we do *not* write *the cars's wheels*.
That would sound silly. It also looks silly, doesn't it? There are *too many*
S sounds.

What we do in this case is to put in the *apostrophe* and omit the extra *s*.
Cars's becomes *cars'* (no extra *s*).

EXERCISE 1:

The hands are pointing at the *cats'*
whiskers.
As you can see, there are *two* cats.
Notice we do not write *cats's*.

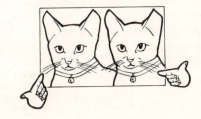

Write out in your exercise book, just as in the example on page 13, which parts of the cats are being pointed at in the following pictures.

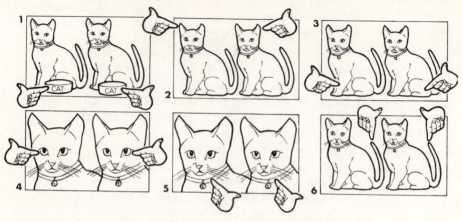

Check with the answers on page 132.

EXERCISE 2

Write out the following list in your exercise book, as shown below, filling in the blanks by using the apostrophe instead of the longer phrase.

This is what you should write

Without the apostrophe The tips of the leaves	Using the apostrophe The leaves' tips

Without the apostrophe

1. The backs of the horses
2. The blazers of the schoolboys
3. The shops belonging to the grocers
4. The hats which the old ladies were wearing
5. The bus carrying the supporters
6. For the sake of goodness
7. The bonnets of the pipers
8. The elbows of the fiddlers
9. The bells of the churches
10. The corks of the bottles
11. The Chief Constables of the cities

Check with the answers on page 132.

EXERCISE 3

Write out the following story in your exercise book, putting in the apostrophe wherever it is needed. Make sure you put the apostrophe in the correct place.

This was the day Wendy dreaded more than any other. The department stores doors were still closed but already a large crowd had gathered outside. Wendy looked around her. What a mess it all seemed! The shop was a jumble of ladies hats and coats, girls dresses, gents socks and ties, boys jerseys. She remembered her mothers warning and put her bag well out of sight under the counter. It wouldnt be the first time that a customer walked away with an assistants handbag thinking it was for sale.

She looked at the clock. In two minutes time the doors would burst open and a flood of people pour in. She tried to remember Mr Laidlaws instructions about dealing with customers disputes.

> *Show this completed exercise to your teacher*

EXERCISE 4

Finish off this story for yourself by telling what happened when the customers actually arrived.

> *Show your completed story to your teacher*

Unit 3 Using the apostrophe when letters are missed out

In our writing, especially in letters and in stories, we sometimes join certain words together and *shorten* them by missing out *one* or *more* letters. When we do this, we use the *apostrophe* to show that there is *one* letter or *more than one* letter missing.

Unit Test

Write these sentences putting in the apostrophe correctly.

1. Im not sure where I put it.
2. Theres a gale warning on the radio.
3. Were late for school!

4. Shouldnt you take out the plug first?
5. Cant you see what Im doing?
6. Hes one of the best goalkeepers in the country.

> *Now check with the answers on page 132.*
> *If you made no mistakes, report to your teacher.*
> *If you made any mistakes, continue with this unit.*

Here are a few examples

I am shortened to *I'm*

Note *two* words are joined into *one*. The *apostrophe* is to show that the *a* is missing.

I am = I ⱥ'm

There is can be shortened to *there's*

Again *one* word. The *apostrophe* replaces the letter *i* which is left out.

There is = *there ɨ's*

Is not can be shortened to *isn't*

One word. The letter missing here is *o*.

Is not = *isn'ⱥt*

EXERCISE 1

Write out the following lists in your exercise book, as shown below, and fill in the blanks.

Full Expression	Shortened Form	Full Expression	Shortened Form
1. there is	there's	7. –	you'll
2. I am	I'm	8. –	haven't
3. is not	isn't	9. –	where's
4. were not	–	10. –	what's
5. that is	–	11. we are	–
6. should not	–	12. –	they're

16

Full Expression	Shortened Form	Full Expression	Shortened Form
13. I shall/will	–	17. –	hadn't
14. are not	–	18. you would	–
15. we shall/will	–	19. I had	–
16. –	wouldn't	20. who is	–

Check with the answers on page 133.

EXERCISE 2

Write out the following sentences in your exercise book putting in the missing apostrophes.

1. Whos your friend?
2. Hes no friend of mine; thats my brother.
3. Whos been eating my porridge?
4. Its that girl from next door again!
5. Id walk a million miles for one of your smiles.
6. Youll never walk alone.
7. Whod have believed it?
8. Heres your hat. Whats your hurry?
9. I wouldn't like to be in your shoes.
10. Theyre all Ive got.

Check with the correct answers on page 133.

EXERCISE 3

Everybody has heard of the Fly-in-the-Soup jokes.
Example: Q. "Waiter, what's this fly doing in my soup?"
*   A. "It's doing the breast-stroke, sir."*

You must know some of your own. In your exercise book, write out the following questions and put in answers of your own.

1. Q. "Waiter, what's this fly doing in my soup?"
   A. —

2. Q. "Waiter, there's a fly in my soup!"
   A. —

3. Q. "Waiter, there's a fly in my soup!"
   A. —

Show your completed sentences to your teacher.

The Sentence, or Period: Space: Capital

It was obvious that Cyril Davies had only a few moments of life left.

Inspector Hutcheson of the Yard leaned over him. "Who was it, sir? Who gave you the poisoned cup of tea?"

Cyril Davies made a last effort. His eyes bulging, he tried to sit up in bed.

"It was. . . ."

The faces of those round the bed were white with dread.

"It was . . . was. . . ."

But the effort had killed him. He fell back on the bed without saying another word. We shall never know whether his wife, the butler or either of his two nephews had delivered the fatal dose.

"It was. . . ."

This is an *uncompleted* sentence. It doesn't tell us very much, does it? You could not use this sentence as evidence in court.

Obviously, Cyril Davies intended to finish the sentence. Perhaps he was going to say *"It was my wife."* Or maybe he was about to say *"It was the butler."*

Now these are *real* sentences. They are *completed*. They *tell* us something. If you used either of *these* sentences in court, you would have a better chance of a conviction.

Sentences are the building blocks of a language. No doubt people at first spoke in single words, as babies still do when they are first learning to speak.

Later we learn to put words together to form blocks of meaning which we call *Sentences*. *Sentences* can be of any size from one or two words up to a hundred and more! However, *all* sentences make *sense* on their own.

Unit 1 Capital Letters and Full Stops

When we write sentences down, we always begin the sentence with a *Capital Letter* and we always end a sentence with a *full stop* – or *Period*.

Example

It was the butler.

| Capital Letter | | Period |

Here are two exercises for you to work through and then show to your teacher.

EXERCISE 1

Below there is a list of uncompleted sentences. In your exercise book, make these sentences complete by adding words of your own. Try to make the complete sentences as interesting as possible. Remember the capital letter and the period at the end. These are most important.

1. My favourite sport is—
2. Coal is—
3. The highest mountain in the world is—
4. Babies are—
5. My best friend looks—
6. The drunken sailor was—
7. Five sixes are—
8. The gorilla who faced him was—
9. —his best friend.
10. —when he got there.
11. The gang hut—
12. Ali Baba thought his luck was in when—
13. Day after day—
14. All mothers—
15. Our teacher is—

EXERCISE 2

Write out the following examples in your exercise book, filling in the blanks with words of your own to make complete *sentences.*

Example Paul felt afraid as he pushed open the heavy, iron gate.

1. My mother—yesterday.
2. School—every day.
3. If—, I would like school.
4. Tomorrow—school team.
5. When I leave school,—
6. Cakes—food.
7. —makes five.
8. A lion, a giraffe and a camel—
9. The ball—fell.
10. The sailing ship—coast.

> *Show these two exercises to your teacher.*

EXERCISE 3

Look at these examples. Could you make up some of your own? Let's try it.
In your exercise book, copy out the examples below and complete them in your own way. Remember the period at the end of the sentence.

1. Agony is—
2. Love is—
3. Summer is—
4. Disappointment is—
5. Kindness is—

6. Football is—
7. Peace is—
8. Contentment is—
9. Winter is—
10. Hate is—

11. Sadness is—
12. Dancing is—
13. Fear is—
14. Heaven is—
15. Home is—

Show your completed sentences to your teacher.

EXERCISE 4

Why not make a wall poster out of one of your sentences from Exercise 3?
All you need is a large sheet of paper and some coloured pens or pencils.

Example

Now make one of your own.

Show your completed poster to your teacher.

The following exercise contains real sentences but the words in each sentence are mixed up. Write them out again, in your exercise book, so that they make sense. Remember to begin each sentence with a capital letter and end with a period.

1. up books teacher open us told our to the
2. fog the caused motorway freezing pile-up the on
3. days told the stay in doctor few me a for to bed
4. idea a Tom brilliant had suddenly
5. asked aircraft to the were passengers board the

Check with the answers on page 134.

Unit 2 Layout

When you want to write more than one sentence, there is something you must be *careful* about.

You must, of course, make sure that your sentences all have a *capital letter* to begin with and that they all end with a *period*. But *between* any two sentences you must leave a *space* so that the reader can easily see that they are different sentences.

Example

        The cat appeared.   The mouse ran away.

When these two sentences come together in **one** piece of writing, here is what they look like:

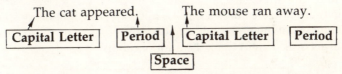

The *space* is very important. It sets your writing out neatly and clearly. It is just as important as the *capital letter* and the *period*.

EXERCISE 1

Rewrite the following sentences in your exercise book, putting in the capital letters, the periods and also the spaces in each example.

1. the lion roared the hyena took off
2. the winger crossed the ball the centre scored

3. i'm Tarzan she is Jane
4. i saw a giraffe it was as big as a house
5. the fire engine raced to the fire the siren was howling
6. seven threes are twenty one seven fours are twenty eight
7. my bicycle was stolen this morning the police have a full description of it
8. there will be rain in northern areas of the country tonight tomorrow will be bright and sunny everywhere

Check with the answers on page 134.

EXERCISE 2

Rewrite the following sentences in your exercise book. Put in the capital letters, the periods and the spaces. (There are three sentences in each example.)

1. the spaceship turned round the laser beam slid past into space the crew breathed a sigh of relief
2. the best football teams have a good manager the manager's job is to buy the players and pick the team it is the trainer's job to make sure the team is fit
3. the hunter stood stock still the rhinoceros looked this way and that with his little pig eyes then he charged
4. i once saw the great Evel Knievel he leapt over fourteen cars on his motor-bike when he landed his bike broke into a million bits and he was lucky to be thrown clear
5. lemmings are tiny creatures a bit like mice they say that every so often large numbers of them commit suicide for no reason by throwing themselves over a cliff i think it's a lot of rubbish myself

Check with the answers on page 134.

EXERCISE 3

The following extracts are all taken from books which you might expect to find in a school library. Perhaps you have read some of these stories for yourself? Rewrite the extracts in your exercise book, putting in capital letters, the periods and the spaces. In each case you are told how many sentences there should be.

1. (3 sentences)

at break Billy went out into the yard the wind cutting straight across from the playing fields made him turn his back and raise a shoulder while he looked around for a sheltered place all the corners were occupied

(*A Kestrel for a Knave* by Barry Hines)

2. (4 sentences)

i went out of doors and looked round the air was pure a cliff on the edge of the aerodrome stood in profile against the sky as if it were daylight over the desert reigned a vast silence as of a house in order

(*Wind, Sand and Stars* by Antoine de Saint-Exupery)

3. (6 sentences)

i got up and wandered as sadly as i could to the door of the church i went inside there were one or two people kneeling in some of the pews i tiptoed down the aisle to nearly the front row and sat in one of the pews myself i didn't kneel but sat with my head bowed i closed my eyes and thought of the vicar coming up and putting his hand on my shoulder and asking me if he could do anything

(*There is a Happy Land* by Keith Waterhouse)

4. (5 sentences)

there were seven puppies in the team the others had been born earlier in the year and were nine and ten months old while White Fang was only eight months old each dog was fastened to the sled by a single rope no two ropes were of the same length while the difference in length between any two ropes was at least that of a dog's body every rope was brought to a ring at the front end of the sled

(*White Fang* by Jack London)

5. (8 sentences)

after some hours the troop reached a lonely hacienda a hacienda is a large farm and being enclosed by a stout high wall it stands up like a small fortress in the country round they rode into the spacious farm yard and dismounted in order to rest themselves a bit the owner of the hacienda came out and the officer asked whether he had seen anything of a party of mounted men the man declared that no one could have ridden past the place without his knowing it whereupon the officer informed him that he would have to search the hacienda and the owner replied that he might do as he liked and went back into the house the troopers were about to follow him when they were met by a volley from different parts of the house by the time they had retreated through the yard gates they had four wounded and one dead

(The Treasure of the Sierra Madre by B. Traven)*

> Check with the answers on pages 135–6.

Unit 3 Comma Splice and Capital Letters

Unit Test – Comma splice

Rewrite these sentences correctly. There are two sentences in each example.

1. George looked at his watch, it was twenty past nine.
2. An upstairs door banged shut, outside the wind howled.
3. Sheila decided not to buy the oranges in the supermarket, they were cheaper in the corner shop.
4. My mother accused me of lying to her, I did not know what she would do next.
5. The driver pressed his foot hard on the brake-pedal, his taxi was completely out of control.
6. The nurse told me not to worry about the operation, her smile cheered me up for the rest of the day.

> Check with the answers on page 136.
> If you have made no mistakes, move on to Capital Letters, page 26.
> If you have made any mistakes, continue with this unit.

It is a very common mistake in writing sentences, to put a *comma* where a *period* is actually required. This is sometimes caused by the writer's thoughts and ideas racing ahead of his or her actual handwriting. At other times, the writer feels that some sort of pause is required and puts in a *comma*.

If a *period* is written down, instead of a *comma*, the chances are that it will be correct nine times out of ten when a pause is required.

Example Slowly he pulled himself up on the river-bank, his clothes were sopping wet.

this should be

Slowly he pulled himself up on the river-bank. His clothes were sopping wet.

This mistake is called the *Comma Splice*.

If you make this mistake in your writing, a good tip is to read through your writing slowly so that it makes sense to you. If you make a definite pause in your reading and you have written a comma, then you should change it to a period. Of course, if there is not even a comma when you have a pause in your reading, you must decide whether it requires a *comma* or a *period*. (See Comma Module, Unit 3, page 77.)

EXERCISE 1

Write out the following sentences in your exercise book changing the comma splice *to a period. Remember, a capital letter always follows a* period.

1. We waited outside the cinema for a long time, finally the others arrived.
2. What did you do last night, I stayed at home.
3. I decided to buy a new pair of shoes, my brother said he would advise me.
4. Cigarettes can damage your health, they can also shorten your life.
5. Sharon chuckled as she read her horoscope, it seemed to be her lucky day.
6. Although I did not know her name, I recognised the old lady, she lived near our school.
7. I buy cassettes instead of records, they are more expensive but not so easily damaged as records.
8. Trevor hurled the stick into the middle of the pond, his dog splashed happily after it.
9. The volcano erupted without any warning, many islanders were killed before they could be rescued.
10. He pleaded with me for a long time, finally I gave in.

> Show this exercise to your teacher.

EXERCISE 2

Write out the following passages in your exercise book, changing the comma splices to periods.

1. We jumped out of the aircraft at midnight, my parachute opened easily and I could see the others drifting silently towards the ground, there was a full moon and I could make out white markers quite clearly below me in the field, there were a number of people running out of a small wood to greet us, they were waving their arms in the air.

2. Many people find it difficult to write in proper sentences, they often forget to put a capital letter at the beginning of a sentence and a period at the end of a sentence, this means their writing is confused and it does not always make sense.

3. With a telephone you can chat to friends and make last minute arrangements, you can keep in touch with your family, make bookings, ring the shops and call the plumber or electrician at the first sign of trouble. Then, of course, other people can ring you, most of their calls will be friendly chats but sometimes a message can be vital, it's then that a phone can save you hours of frustration, a wasted journey or missed appointment.

(Post Office publication)

Check with the answers on page 136.

Unit Test – Capital Letters

Rewrite the following sentences correctly in your exercise book.

1. i hope to go on holiday to spain next year.
2. my dog goldie had pups last november.
3. glasgow is situated on the river clyde.
4. our teacher read to us from treasure island by robert louis stevenson.
5. last sunday we visited our cousins in newcastle.
6. the rosewell youth club meets every monday and friday, except in the holiday months of july and august.

Check with the answers on page 137.
If you made no mistakes move on to the Supplementary Exercises on page 28.
If you made any mistakes, continue with this unit.

You have already used *Capital Letters* at the beginning of sentences but there are other words which must always begin with a *Capital Letter*. These are always the *Name* of *Something* or *Someone*.

Example

Days of the Week
    Monday
    Saturday

Months of the Year
    April
    December

People's Names
    Samantha
    Mr Brown

Place Names
    San Francisco
    Wembley Stadium

Organisations
    BBC
    Phoenix Youth Club

The First and Main Words in Book Titles
    Jaws
    Moby Dick
    Lord of the Flies

EXERCISE 1

Write out these sentences in your exercise book, using capital letters where you think they are necessary.

1. in 1980, the olympic games were held in moscow.
2. when i was on holiday in new york last september, i was able to visit the united nations building.
3. sally and james flanagan organised a dance in aid of oxfam.
4. we have a copy of the oxford english dictionary in our school library.
5. hank fielding's song, golden corn, appeared in the top twenty three weeks running.
6. next tuesday i have an appointment with mr foster who is the area manager for smith and jones.
7. watership down is an unusual story about rabbits which has been translated into many languages.
8. thirty days hath september, april, june and november.

9. aunt margaret introduced me to her neighbours, the thomsons, when i visited her last thursday.
10. the queen narrowly missed injury when her official car skidded into a lamp-post on waterloo bridge this morning.

Check with the answers on page 137.

EXERCISE 2

Write out these lists in your exercise book, remembering to use capital letters.

1. A list of *five* boys names.
2. A list of *five* girls names.
3. A list of *five* surnames.
4. A list of *five* British rivers.
5. A list of *five* European cities.
6. A list of *five* record titles.
7. A list of *five* schools in your area.
8. A list of *five* brand names of sweets.
9. A list of *five* months of the year.
10. A list of *five* TV personalities.

Show your lists to your teacher.

SUPPLEMENTARY EXERCISES

1. Write *four* sentences about the room you are working in at present. (Think about the people; the view; the furniture; the decoration.)
2. Write *three* sentences about *today's* weather.
3. Write *four* sentences about a favourite TV programme which you watch regularly. (Name; type of programme; why you enjoy it; who appears in it.)
4. Write *five* sentences describing one of your *close* friends. (Think about name; age and height; hair colour; clothes; interests.)
5. Write *as many sentences as you can* on your special interest or hobby. When you have finished, count your sentences and put the number in brackets at the foot of the page.

Show these exercises to your teacher.

MODULE 3

Spelling One

Unit 1

INTRODUCTION

To get the most out of this section on spelling, you will need:

1. A good dictionary.
2. An exercise book.
3. A notebook in which you will write down all the words which give you difficulty. This will grow into your personal spelling dictionary.

1. Why do you need a dictionary?

You need a dictionary when you are working at your spelling, because it is a great deal easier to remember how to spell a word if you know what it means. Take every opportunity you can to look up words in your dictionary.

In this way, you will learn how a dictionary works – and this is a very valuable skill for a student. You will also begin to realise that even the most difficult words are made up of parts of words which you already know! Consider, for example, how many words end in -*ing* or -*ment* or begin with *dis-* or *in-*.

Moreover, by getting into the habit of looking up new words in the dictionary, you will improve your vocabulary immensely.

2. The exercise book

This will be your general work book in Spelling. In this book, you will write out all the exercises which are set out for you in the spelling units which follow. Also in this book you write down any new words you meet. Most important of all, in this book you must write down all those words in which you made a spelling mistake, in any school subject or in any part of your ordinary classwork.

In this way, you will begin to discover for yourself what your own special spelling problems are. Once you know what they are, you will be able to work on them and so improve your spelling.

3. Your spelling dictionary

This is most important if you want to be a good speller. All you need to do to make a notebook into a spelling dictionary is to arrange the pages in alphabetical order. Each time you meet a new word, or discover a mistake in your spelling, first of all correct the spelling and then write the correctly spelt word down in its proper place in your dictionary.

What makes this particular spelling dictionary special is the fact that it is *yours* and *yours alone*. It will include all the words which *you* are learning how to use in your writing and all the words you are having trouble in spelling.

Just by running your eye through your spelling dictionary every so often you will learn to spell, without any trouble, all those words which you need in your writing.

How do these units and modules work?
The basic plan behind this spelling scheme is:

(a) To draw the students' attention to the fact that words are made up of *elements*, that is parts of words or clusters of letters, which crop up again and again in English and which become easy to recognise and remember.

(b) To outline those few rules of spelling which can be useful to a learner.

(c) To give the student as much *practice* as possible in writing out and becoming thoroughly familiar with those words which he or she is struggling to master.

How have the words in these units been chosen?
The words contained in the following exercises are based on thorough research into students' writing.* They represent the words most frequently used by young people in their writing as well as those words most frequently spelt wrong.

Our list of words to be practised has been sub-divided as follows:

1. Words which can be spelt according to stated rules; *ie, ei* is an example.
2. Words which contain common letter clusters, such as *ou, au, ss, cc, ght*.
3. Words which have common endings and suffixes. Such endings, which are plentiful in English, include *-ment, -able, -ible, -ary* and many others.

* *Alphabetical Spelling List,* 1963 (Wheaton, Exeter)
  The University Spelling Book, 1955 (Prentice-Hall, USA)
  Key Words to Literacy, 1968 (Ladybird, Loughborough)

As a result of this sub-division, under each heading there are a comparatively small number of words for you to learn in each unit or part of a unit. If you learned all these words you would end up with a very large number of highly useful words at your command. You would almost certainly be a very good speller!

A useful spelling list containing all the words practised in these modules is given at the end of this book for easy reference and further practice.

VOWEL CLUSTERS – *ie, ei*

1

i comes before *e* except after *c* when the sound of the letters is *ee* as in the word bee.

In all the following words the sound is *ee*. As this sound does *not* follow *c*, the spelling is *ie*.

believe	achievement	piece	thief	fiercely
chief	relieved	yield	field	

Two important exceptions to this rule are seize *and* weird.

1. *Write out this list of words in your exercise book.*
2. *Now write the words out in your spelling dictionary. Remember to put them on the proper page.*

Here are two exercises for you to work through and then show to your teacher.

EXERCISE 1

Write out the following sentences in your exercise book, filling in the blanks with the words from the box above.

1. "Do you b – – – – – e in God?" she asked him f – – – – – – y.

2. The t – – – f was very r – – – – – – d when the policeman walked past the door.

3. To swim the English Channel is a great a – – – – – – – – – t.

4. This f – – – d has an annual y – – – d of twelve tonnes of potatoes.

5. The c – – – f engineer wiped his brow with an oily rag.

31

6. The yachtsman was very r – – – – – – d when the coastline came into view.

7. The film I saw last night was called "The T – – – f of Baghdad."

8. Her mother gave her two ham sandwiches and a p – – – e of cake to take to the picnic.

EXERCISE 2

Make up sentences of your own using the words given to you below. Write the completed sentences in your exercise book. Make your sentences as interesting as you can.

1. relieved   field
2. thief   chief
3. fiercely   believed
4. achievement   piece

5. field   chief
6. believe   weird
7. relieved   yield
8. seized   thief

> *Show your completed sentences to your teacher.*
> *Look back over any other writing you have been doing in class. If you have made any mistakes with these words, correct them and put them in your spelling dictionary.*

In the following words the sound is *ee* and it follows *c* so the spelling is *ei*.

perc*ei*ve	rec*ei*ve	dec*ei*ve
conc*ei*ved	c*ei*ling	conc*ei*ted

1. *Write out this list of words in your exercise book.*
2. *Now write the words out in their proper place in your spelling dictionary.*

Here are two exercises for you to work through and then show to your teacher.

EXERCISE 3

Write out the following sentences in your exercise book, filling in the blanks with words from the box above.

1. It is very wicked to d – – – – – e your mother.

2. Maureen was clever but nobody liked her as she was also very
c – – – – – – – d.

3. The leader of the gang c – – – – – – – d a plan for their escape.

4. Looking up at the c – – – – – g, the fat man said, "I p – – – – – – e that
you have water leaking from the floor above.

5. Dr Wilson went to Stockholm to r – – – – – e the Nobel Prize.

6. Do my eyes d – – – – – e me or is that cat four feet tall?

7. It is better to give than to r – – – – – e.

8. The last time our upstairs neighbours had a party, a piece of the
c – – – – – g fell on top of my Dad as he was watching television.

EXERCISE 4

*Make up sentences of your own using the words given to you below. Write
the completed sentence in your exercise book. Be careful with the spelling
of these words.*

1. received   piece
2. ceiling
3. fiercely
4. field

5. deceive   thief
6. conceited
7. chief
8. believed

> *Show your completed sentences to your teacher.*

3

When the sound is *not ee*, then normally you have *ei*. Here are some
examples.

*ei*ther	n*ei*ther	*ei*ght	n*ei*ghbour	l*ei*sure
for*ei*gn	w*ei*ght	h*ei*ght	th*ei*r	

Two important exceptions to this rule are the words
view and friend.

1. *Write out this list, including the two exceptions, in your exercise book.*
2. *Now write the words out in your spelling dictionary. Make sure that you
put them in their proper place.*

Here are two exercises for you to work through and then show to your teacher.

EXERCISE 5

Write out the following sentences in your exercise book filling in the blanks from the list you have just written out.

1. E – – – – r go or else stay, but make up your mind.

2. N – – – – – r my brother nor I was ever involved in mischief at school.

3. My young sister is the same h – – – – t as I am and I am two years older!

4. Have you ever been in a f – – – – – n country?

5. Ny n – – – – – – – r has e – – – t dogs and two cats.

6. The two girls left t – – – r bikes by the side door.

7. The holiday crowds drifted home at t – – – r l – – – – – e.

8. "E – – – t and e – – – t do not make eighteen!" yelled our new teacher.

9. The v – – w from my f – – – – d's front window is quite marvellous.

10. Though Joan is my best f – – – – d, we sometimes quarrel.

EXERCISE 6

Make up sentences of your own using the words given below and write them in your exercise book.

1. eighty	neighbour		5. either	
2. height	weight		6. view	neither
3. friends	their		7. leisure	
4. foreign			8. their	neighbours

Show your completed exercises to your teacher.
Look back over any writing you have been doing in class. If you have made any spelling mistakes, correct them and put them in the proper place in your spelling dictionary.

Unit 2

CONSONANT CLUSTERS – *ch, tch, ck*

1

ch is a combination of letters which is common in English. Here is a list of some of the more difficult examples.

*Ch*ristmas	*ch*imney	*ch*ildren
*ch*ocolate	mis*ch*ief	sandwi*ch*
stoma*ch*	*ch*urch	whi*ch*

1. *Write out this list of words in your exercise book.*
2. *Now write the words out in your spelling dictionary.*

EXERCISE 7

Write out the following sentences in your exercise book, filling in the blanks with words from the box.

1. Each C – – – – – – – s I hang my stocking near the c – – – – – y.

2. My friend likes to lie on her s – – – – – h while she is reading.

3. All c – – – – – – n like c – – – – – – – e, especially at
   C – – – – – – – s.

4. I would rather have a s – – – – – – h than a piece of cake.

5. W – – – h would you rather have, a cake of c – – – – – – – e or a box
   on the ears?

6. In the olden days, c – – – – – – n used to have to climb down
   c – – – – – ys to clean them.

7. You cannot eat a s – – – – – – h in c – – – – h. It would not be right.

8. The c – – – – – – n always stop their m – – – – – – f just before
   C – – – – – – – s.

Show your completed sentences to your teacher

35

2 Another common consonant cluster is *tch*. Here are some examples.

| witch | ditch | kitchen | scratch | butcher | catch |

1. *Write this list out in your exercise book.*
2. *Now write the words out in alphabetical order in your spelling dictionary.*

Here are two exercises for you to work through and then show to your teacher.

EXERCISE 8

Write out the following sentences in your exercise book, filling in the blanks with words from the box above.

1. He bought some cold meat from the b – – – – – r to make sandwiches for their picnic.

2. When he fell into the d – – – h, my uncle received only a s – – – – – h.

3. The c – – – h on our k – – – – – n door does not work properly.

4. If I saw a real w – – – h, I would run a mile!

5. Every Christmas the b – – – – – r sends us a huge turkey.

6. My cat likes to s – – – – – h itself in front of the fire.

EXERCISE 9

Using the words which you are given below, make up some sentences of your own and write them out in your exercise book.

1. ditch   Christmas
2. catch   mischief
3. stomach   kitchen
4. witch   chimney

5. sandwich   children
6. scratch   church
7. butcher   chocolate
8. chimney   ditch

| *Show these completed exercises to your teacher.* |

3 Another common letter cluster in our language is *ck*. Here are some
examples.

| chicken | picked | cricket | ticket | bucket | crack |

1. *Write out this list of words in your exercise book.*
2. *Now write them into their proper place in your spelling dictionary.*

*Here are two exercises for you to work through and then show to
your teacher*

EXERCISE 10

*Write out the following sentences in your exercise book, filling in the blanks
with words from the box above.*

1. Her mother gently p – – – – d a c – – – – – n out of the basket.

2. What I like most about c – – – – – t is the c – – – k of ball on bat.

3. For Christmas I was given a t – – – – t for the circus.

4. The c – – – – – n was delicious when made up into sandwiches.

5. After the storm, my Dad discovered a c – – – k in the kitchen chimney.

6. The b – – – – t in our classroom is usually full of crisp bags, chewing
   gum and pencil shavings.

7. My big brother went mad when he found a scratch on his beloved
   c – – – – – t bat.

8. Because her office was near the theatre, Marilyn p – – – – d up her
   brother's t – – – – t for the concert.

EXERCISE 11

Using the words listed below, make up sentences of your own and write them in your exercise book.

1. chicken	Christmas	5. ticket	neighbour
2. picked	piece	6. cricket	height	weight
3. thief	bucket	7. mischief	children	chicken
4. ceiling	crack	8. picked	bucket	ticket

> *Show these completed exercises to your teacher.*
> *Look back over any other writing you have been doing in class. Make a list of the words you have misspelled in your exercise book. Remember to put these words into your spelling dictionary.*

Unit 3

WORD ENDINGS -*ary*, -*ery*

Endings are among the parts of words which you can learn to recognise. In this unit, we are going to look at two common endings -*ary* and -*ery*.

The ending -*ary* is found in a large number of words which you will often use. Here are the most common ones:

diction*ary*	prim*ary*	second*ary*
secret*ary*	necess*ary*	milit*ary*
Janu*ary*	Febru*ary*	libr*ary*

1. *Write out this list of words in your exercise book.*
2. *Now write the words out in the spelling dictionary which you are building. Remember to put them in their proper place.*

Here are two exercises for you to work through and then show to your teacher.

EXERCISE 12

Write out the following sentences in your exercise book, filling in the blanks from the list above.

1. When I started at the s – – – – – – – y school, I was given a
d – – – – – – – – y of my own.

2. Last F – – – – – – y I was off school with severe stomach pains.

3. One of the things Jenny liked about living near the Palace was watching
the m – – – – – – y parades.

4. J – – – – – y is a terrible month; there is nothing to look forward to.

5. At my first p – – – – – y school I was taught how to use the
l – – – – – y.

6. If you lose your dinner-ticket in our school it is n – – – – – – – y to see
the s – – – – – – y about buying a new one.

7. A good d – – – – – – – – y is n – – – – – – – y for a student.

8. When I am spelling it, I nearly always miss out the first 'r' in the word
F – – – – – – y!

9. Remember in the word 'n – – – – – – – y' there is only one 'c'!

10. I would like to be a s – – – – – – – y in a Public L – – – – – y when I
leave school.

EXERCISE 13

Using the words below, make up eight sentences of your own and write them out in your exercise book.

1. dictionary   which   Christmas
2. secretary   foreign
3. leisure   January
4. military   friends

5. either   January   February
6. necessary   field
7. library   necessary
8. secondary   primary

Show these exercises to your teacher.

2

Here is a list of the commonest words which have the ending *-ery*.

ba*kery*	ce*lery*	sce*nery*	embroi*dery*
machi*nery*	my*stery*	jewel*lery*	

1. *Write out this list of words in your exercise book.*
2. *Now write the words out in their proper alphabetical order in your spelling dictionary.*

Here are two exercises for you to work through and then show to your teacher.

EXERCISE 14

Write out the following sentences, filling in the blanks from the list you have just been given.

1. They have installed new m – – – – – – – y in the b – – – – y down the road.

2. It was a perfect m – – – – – y where the j – – – – – – – y had gone.

3. The s – – – – – y of the West Highlands of Scotland is famous all over the world.

4. Because she is fond of sewing, my sister was given an e – – – – – – – – – y set for Christmas. What she really wanted was a tracksuit!

5. At midnight the s – – – – – y had an air of m – – – – – y.

6. If there is one thing I can't stand it is those c – – – – y sticks my Mum insists on buying.

7. Mr Brown's b – – – – y is right next door to the butcher's shop

8. I wouldn't mind working in a j – – – – – – – y shop.

EXERCISE 15

Make up sentences of your own using the words given to you below and write them down in your exercise book. Make them as interesting as you can.

1. mystery   machinery
2. bakery
3. scenery   January
4. embroidery

5. jewellery
6. mystery   celery
7. machinery
8. scenery   neighbours

> *Show these exercises to your teacher.*

3 Here are two words which look quite alike and *sound the same,* yet it is important that you should be able to tell the difference between them.

> stationary   stationery

Look up the word stationary *in the dictionary. Write the word down in your exercise book along with its meaning.*

Now look up the word stationery. *Write this word in your exercise book along with its meaning.*

EXERCISE 16

Write out the following sentences in your exercise book, filling in the blanks with either stationary *or* stationery.

1. The car was s – – – – – – – y at the kerb-side.

2. A good secretary always has a full supply of office s – – – – – – – y.

3. We bought special s – – – – – – – y for my sister's wedding last summer.

4. Someone ran into us while we were s – – – – – – – y at the lights.

5. S – – – – – – – y includes paper and envelopes.

> *Now check your answers with those on page 138.*

MODULE 4

Spelling Two

Unit 1

ADDING ENDINGS

Words ending with a *consonant* preceded by a *single vowel, double* the *consonant* before adding an *ending which starts with a vowel.*

Here is one example.

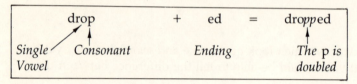

Here is another example using a word with two syllables

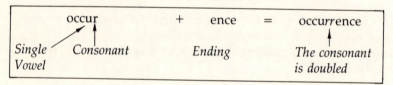

EXERCISE 1

Write out the list which follows in your exercise book, filling in the blanks correctly. The first one is done for you.

	Word	Ending	New
1.	sad	est	saddest
2.	begin	ing	—
3.	refer	ing	—
4.	equal	ed	—
5.	prefer	ing	—
6.	model	ed	—
7.	jewel	ery	—
8.	regret	able	—
9.	occur	ence	—
10.	pencil	ed	—

	Word	Ending	New
11.	begin	er	–
12.	model	ing	–
13.	regret	ed	–
14.	occur	ing	–
15.	prefer	ed	–

Check with the answers on page 139.
1. If you made any mistakes correct them.
2. Write out the words above in your spelling dictionary.
   Remember to put them on the proper page.

EXERCISE 2

Write out the following sentences in your exercise book, filling in the blanks with words from the previous exercise.

1. Last year my big brother e – – – – – – d the World High Jump Record.

2. I did not know that you were r – – – – – – – g to me.

3. Our Art teacher is showing us how to make our own j – – – – – – – y out of beads and scraps of silver.

4. The waiter asked me if I p – – – – – – – d dessert or biscuits and cheese.

5. Mary always r – – – – – – d that she had left the pop group now that they were world famous.

6. My brother, Michael, seems to spend most of his life up to the elbows in m – – – – – – – g clay.

7. My mother hates it, if she misses the b – – – – – – – g of a play on TV.

8. Fights are a nightly o – – – – – – – – e in our neighbourhood.

Show this exercise to your teacher.

Note There are two important exceptions to this rule – *happen* and *benefit*.
When you add *-ing* and *-ed* to these words, you *do not* double the *final consonant*. (See page 44.)

happen	+	ed	=	happened
happen	+	ing	=	happening
benefit	+	ed	=	benefited
benefit	+	ing	=	benefiting

1. Write these four words out in your exercise book.
2. Copy them out into your spelling dictionary.

EXERCISE 3

Make up sentences of your own using the words given to you and copy them into your exercise book.

1. happened   field
2. regretted   decision
3. benefited   friends
4. preferred

5. happening   kitchen
6. modelled   statue
7. occurred
8. jewellery

> Show this exercise to your teacher.

EXERCISE 4

Write out the following list of words in your exercise book, filling in the blanks where they occur.

Word	Ending -ed	Ending -ing
1. equal	equalled	—
2. happen	—	happening
3. model	—	—
4. prefer	—	preferring
5. regret	regretted	—
6. occur	—	—
7. benefit	—	—
8. refer	—	—

> Look up the answers on page 139.
> If you have made any mistakes correct them.

Unit 2

There are a very large number of words in English which have *ea* in them. Here are some of the more important ones.

alrea dy	breakfast	instead	really
beneath	increase	jealous	measles
wealthy	appearance	pleasure	peace

1. *Write this list out in your exercise book.*
2. *Now write the words in their proper place in your spelling dictionary.*

Here are two exercises for you to work through and then show to your teacher.

EXERCISE 1

Write out the following sentences in your exercise book, filling in the blanks from the list given above.

1. I – – – – – d of eating b – – – – – – – t, my Dad goes jogging every morning.

2. We were a – – – – – y late before we left for the concert.

3. From the length of time she spends in front of the mirror, it is obvious that my sister takes great p – – – – – – e in her a – – – – – – – – e.

4. It seems easy for w – – – – – y people to i – – – – – – e their fortunes.

5. M – – – – – s is a very unsightly illness.

6. I am r – – – – y keen on fishing.

7. If there is one thing I can't stand, it is people who are j – – – – – s.

8. This is Rocky's first a – – – – – – – – e in this country and every concert is a sell-out.

45

EXERCISE 2

Make up sentences of your own, using the words you are given, and write them in your exercise book.

1. wealthy
2. beneath   ocean
3. increase
4. pleasure   beach

5. jealous
6. measles
7. appearance
8. already   breath

> *Show these exercises to your teacher.*

CONSONANT CLUSTERS – *cc, wh, th*

There are a large number of words with *cc* in them. Here are some of them.

accident	account	soccer	occasion	occupation
succeed	accumulated	tobacco	occurred	successful

1. *Write out this list in your exercise book.*
2. *Write the words into your spelling dictionary.*

Here are two exercises for you to work through and then show to your teacher.

EXERCISE 3

Write the following sentences out in your exercise book, filling in the blanks from the list above.

1. When I had my a – – – – – – t, I was taken to the Royal Infirmary.

2. If at first you don't s – – – – – d, try again.

3. During his travels in the East, my uncle Carl a – – – – – – – – – d a vast fortune.

4. On the o – – – – – – n of my birthday, I was given a s – – – – r game.

5. My grandfather said that he gave up t – – – – – o when he was a young man.

6. It never o – – – – – – d to my sister to help me with my homework.

46

7. On a – – – – – t of his bad chest, my cousin had to give up boxing.

8. Some day, I would like to be s – – – – – – – l in business.

EXERCISE 4

Make up sentences of your own using the words given to you below and write them into your exercise book.

1. successful
2. occasion
3. occurred
4. account   butcher

5. occupation
6. accident
7. accumulated
8. succeed

> *Show these exercises to your teacher.*

2 *wh* is a very common cluster in English. Here are some examples which you should learn to recognise and spell.

*wh*eat	*wh*istle	*wh*ispered	*wh*ole
*wh*ile	*wh*ich	*wh*ere	*wh*o
*wh*ether	mean*wh*ile	some*wh*ere	every*wh*ere

1. *Write this list out in your exercise book.*
2. *Now write them out in your spelling dictionary. Remember to put them in their proper place.*

Here are two exercises for you to work through and show to your teacher.

EXERCISE 5

Write out the following sentences in your exercise book, filling in the blanks from the list above.

1. W – – – e are the people w – o were supposed to help us today?

2. M – – – – – – – e all my w – – – t crop is rotting in the fields.

3. He w – – – – – – – d to me, "W – – – e are we?"

4. If you w – – – – – e loudly enough, the dog will come back.

5. She takes her dog with her e – – – – – – – – e she goes.

6. I don't know w – – – – – r the thieves will return or not.

7. W – – – h is your favourite team?

8. I once ate a w – – – e joint of beef!

EXERCISE 6

Make up sentences of your own using the words given below. Write the sentences into your exercise book.

1. meanwhile   ranch
2. who   believed
3. whatever
4. which   studying

5. whistle   happiness
6. whisper
7. wheat   yields
8. whole   somewhere

| Show these exercises to your teacher. |

3 Here is a list of *some* words which have the cluster *th* in them.

another	further	weather	thousand
thought	healthy	therefore	although
altogether	there	their	strength

1. *Write out this list in your exercise book.*
2. *Put these words into their proper place in your spelling dictionary.*

Here are two exercises for you to work through and then show to your teacher.

EXERCISE 7

Write out the following sentences in your exercise book, filling in the blanks from the list given above.

1. The w – – – – – r improved, so they put on t – – – r light summer clothing.

2. A – – – – – h he had the strength of ten men, his wife could tame him easily.

3. On the top of the hill, t – – – e was a bonfire.

4. Everyone in our street t – – – – – t that our dog Mickey, was a nuisance. Except us, of course!

5. If you want to stay h – – – – – y, you should eat plenty of greens.

6. The winning horse drew f – – – – – r and f – – – – – r away from the others.

7. They put a – – – – – r pint of oil in t – – – r car.

8. T – – – e were three t – – – – – – d people in the concert hall last night.

EXERCISE 8

Make sentences of your own, using the words below.

1. therefore   strength
2. there
3. healthy   although
4. altogether

5. another   sausage
6. their   dictionaries
7. therefore   appearance
8. thought   successful

> Show these exercises to your teacher.
> Look back through the other pieces of writing you have been doing and put into your spelling dictionary all those words which you have spelled incorrectly.

Unit 3

WORD ENDING -*y*

1

Forming plurals from words ending in *y*. When words end in *y*, the plural is formed by changing the *y* to an *i* and adding *es*.

Here is an example.

Singular	Plural
family	families
ends in *y*	*y* becomes *i* and add *es*

EXERCISE 9

In your exercise book, write out the following list in two columns – one for the singular and one for the plural. The first example shows you how to do this.

Singular	Plural	Singular	Plural
1. lorry	lorries	9. duty	—
2. city	—	10. industry	—
3. boundary	—	11. memory	—
4. community	—	12. quality	—
5. cherry	—	13. quantity	—
6. dictionary	—	14. century	—
7. butterfly	—	15. family	—
8. library	—		

> Check with the answers on page 139.
> If you have made any mistakes, correct them and write the singular and plural forms into your spelling dictionary in their proper place.

EXERCISE 10

In the following exercise you are given either the singular or the plural form of the word. Write the whole list out in your exercise book, filling in all the blanks.

Singular	Plural	Singular	Plural
1. lorry	—	5. —	centuries
2. —	families	6. dictionary	—
3. quality	—	7. cherry	—
4. —	memories	8. —	industries

> Check with the answers on page 139.

EXERCISE 11

Make up sentences of your own, using the words given below. Put your completed sentences into your exercise book.

1. boundary   appearance   2. cities   beneath

3. family   measles
4. believe   libraries
5. industry

6. duties   butcher
7. butterflies   field
8. quantities   potatoes

Show this exercise to your teacher.

2 When a word ends in a consonant followed by *y* and you want to add an ending *or suffix* to the word, you change the *y* to an *i*.

Here is an example.

Word	Ending	New Word
busy +	ly	= busily
consonant + y		y *becomes* i

EXERCISE 12

Write out the following table in your exercise book, filling in the blanks as you go along.

1. beauty   + ful   = —
2. noisy   + ly   = —
3. mercy   + less   = —
4. carry   + ed   = —
5. bury   + al   = —
6. marry   + age   = —
7. defy   + ance   = —
8. happy   + ness   = —
9. crafty   + ly   = —
10. mystery + ous   = —

Check with the answers on page 140.

Note The only exception to this rule is when you add *ing* to a word ending in *y*. In this case the *y* stays as it is.

Here is an example

marry +	ing	=	marrying
Ends in *y*	*ing* ending		*y* stays in

EXERCISE 13

Write out the following table in your exercise book, filling in the blanks by adding ing *to the word.*

1.	marry	+	ing	=	—
2.	carry	+	ing	=	—
3.	study	+	ing	=	—
4.	defy	+	ing	=	—
5.	fly	+	ing	=	—

Check with the answers on page 140.

EXERCISE 14

In your exercise book, write out the new words which are formed in the following examples.

1.	mercy	+	less	=	—
2.	carry	+	ing	=	—
3.	try	+	ed	=	—
4.	happy	+	ness	=	—
5.	mystery	+	ous	=	—
6.	fly	+	ing	=	—
7.	likely	+	hood	=	—
8.	study	+	ing	=	—

Check with the answers on page 140.

MODULE 5

Spelling Three

Unit 1

WORD ENDING SILENT -*e*

Words which end in a silent *e* drop the *e* before an ending which starts with a vowel.

Here is an example.

Word	Ending	New Word
write +	ing =	writing
You do not pronounce this *e*. It is silent.	Starts with a vowel *i*.	The *e* is omitted.

EXERCISE 1

In the following exercise, you are asked to join a number of words ending in silent e to a number of different word endings. Write out the new words produced in your exercise book.

1. fame	+	ous	= —	6. excite	+	ing	= —
2. move	+	able	= —	7. value	+	able	= —
3. separate	+	ed	= —	8. believe	+	ed	= —
4. pleasure	+	able	= —	9. receive	+	ed	= —
5. write	+	ing	= —	10. fascinate	+	ing	= —

Check with the answers on page 141.

Note There are a small number of *exceptions* to this rule. They are all words which end in *ge* or *ce* and are followed by *ous* or *able*. In these cases, you keep the *e* in the word.

Here are the most important words involved.

courag*eo*us	chang*ea*ble	notic*ea*ble
advantag*eo*us	peac*ea*ble	

1. *Write this list into your exercise book.*
2. *Now put these words into your spelling dictionary, in their proper place.*

EXERCISE 2

Make up sentences of your own, using the words given you in the following examples. Write the sentences in your exercise book.

1. excitable   field
2. fascinated
3. movable
4. courageous
5. relieved   peaceable

6. changeable
7. writing   advantageous
8. separated
9. accommodation
10. lovable

Show your sentences to your teacher.

Unit 2

VOWEL CLUSTER – *ui*

This can be a tricky combination of letters in English. Fortunately, there are not too many examples to worry about.

Here is a list of the main words involving *ui*.

b*ui*lt	s*ui*t	peng*ui*n	fr*ui*t
n*ui*sance	g*ui*de	j*ui*ce	b*ui*lding

1. *Write out this list in your exercise book.*
2. *Now write the words into your spelling dictionary. Remember to put them in their proper place in the alphabet.*

EXERCISE 3

1. In his confusion, the diner spilt f – – – t j – – – e down his s – – t.
2. "Could you g – – – e me to the pool, please?"

3. It is such a n − − − − − e when it rains on a holiday.

4. The f − − − t bat is a very vicious-looking animal, even if it has a pleasant name.

5. During the earthquake, a great number of people were trapped at the top of the largest b − − − − − g in the city.

6. When you first see a p − − − − − n you would think that it was wearing an evening s − − t!

7. When you are learning to write, the teacher will sometimes g − − − e your hand.

8. Running errands for your parents can be a bit of a n − − − − − − e if you want to watch your favourite television programme.

> Show this exercise to your teacher.

EXERCISE 4

Make up sentences of your own, using the words given below. Write them into your exercise book.

1. fruit butcher	5. guide mountains	
2. penguins	6. suit jacket trousers	
3. built chimney	7. juice bread	
4. nuisance	8. buildings	

> Show this exercise to your teacher.
> Check over your class writing and make a note of your spelling mistakes. Put them into your spelling dictionary after you have corrected them.

CONSONANT CLUSTERS − *sc, ss, mm, mb*

1

Here is a list of a number of commonly used words which have the *sc* cluster in them.

scratch	science	scenery	scarce
conscience	fascinated	escaped	

1. *Write this list in your exercise book.*
2. *Now put the words into your spelling dictionary.*

EXERCISE 5

Write the following exercise in your exercise book, filling in the blanks from the list you have been given above.

1. My Dad said that he was always f – – – – – – – d by s – – – – – e when he was at school.

2. Although my brother cried for ages, he only had a little s – – – – – h on the back of his leg.

3. In our class play I was allowed to move the s – – – – – y.

4. I once knew a man who e – – – – – d from Colditz.

5. When I first went to a pop concert, I was f – – – – – – – – d by the sounds and the flickering lights.

6. It is sometimes difficult to sleep if you have something on your c – – – – – – – – e.

7. The s – – – – – y around our village is very famous.

8. During a power cut, candles become very s – – – – e.

> *Show this exercise to your teacher.*

EXERCISE 6

Make up sentences of your own, using the words you are given in the examples which follow. Write them in your exercise book.

1. science   writing
2. changeable   scenery
3. fascinated   penguins
4. scratched
5. buildings   scene
6. escaped
7. conscience
8. scarce   fruit

> *Show your sentences to your teacher.*

2 There are a large number of words in English which have *ss* in them. Here is a list of some of the most important ones for you to learn.

address	necessary	unless	possible
guess	association	permission	dissatisfied
unnecessary	successful	impossible	

1. Write out this list in your exercise book.
2. Now write them out in your spelling dictionary.

Here are two exercises for you to work through and then show to your teacher.

EXERCISE 7

Write out the following sentences in your exercise book, filling in the blanks from the list above.

1. Our teacher gave us p – – – – – – – – n to leave the room.

2. My a – – – – – s was written in the top right hand corner of the writing paper.

3. It is not p – – – – – – e to be s – – – – – – – – l at sport u – – – – s you practise very hard.

4. I recently joined the Rambling A – – – – – – – – – n, because I have always been fond of walking.

5. It is n – – – – – – – y to have a bell on your bicycle, otherwise the police will stop you.

6. U – – – – s you give up eating so many sweet things, you will lose your teeth.

7. My father was d – – – – – – – – – d with his recent rise in pay.

8. It is i – – – – – – – – e to high-jump two metres if you are only ten years old.

EXERCISE 8

Finish off the following sentences and write them in your exercise book.

1. The Football Association —.   2. In the event of a flood, it is necessary —.

3. If you wish to be successful —.   6. Unless —.
4. Anything is possible if —.   7. A hard hat is necessary when you —.
5. My address —.   8. Guess who —.

> Show these two exercises to your teacher.
> Check over your recent class writing. Make a note of any words which are wrongly spelt. Put these words in your spelling dictionary.

3 Here is a list of some *mm* clusters in words which you will find useful in your writing.

committee	community	commerce	accommodation
immediately	programme	recommend	

1. *Write this list of words out in your exercise book.*
2. *Now write them in your spelling dictionary.*

Here are two exercises for you to work through and then show to your teacher.

EXERCISE 9

Look up each of the following words in a dictionary and write out the word followed by its meaning, in your exercise book.

1. committee   3. programme   5. commerce   7. accommodation
2. immediately   4. recommend   6. community

EXERCISE 10

Make the following examples into sentences by adding words of your own. Write the completed sentences into your exercise book.

1. I became a member of the committee at —.
2. The programme —.
3. Commerce is —.
4. Our community is beginning to —.
5. I recommend —.

6. Immediately after —.
7. Our accommodation during the holidays is —.
8. He arrived immediately —.

Show these exercises to your teacher.

4 Here is a list of words with *mb* in them. Notice that sometimes you pronounce the *b* as in Nove*mb*er, but sometimes you do *not* pronounce the *b* as in cli*mb*.

bo*mb*	cli*mb*	co*mb*	nu*mb*er	cru*mb*s	li*mb*
la*mb*	me*mb*er	reme*mb*er	Nove*mb*er	Dece*mb*er	Septe*mb*er

1. *Write out this list of words in your exercise book.*
2. *Put them into your spelling dictionary in the proper place.*

EXERCISE 11

Write out the following sentences in your exercise book filling in the blanks with words from the list above.

1. Last summer we found an unexploded b – – b in our back garden.

2. My mother always throws c – – – – s into the garden for the birds.

3. I have just become a m – – – – r of our local swimming club.

4. My pal's c – – b has practically no teeth left in it: no wonder his hair is always sticking up in the air.

5. R – – – – – – r, r – – – – – – r the fifth of N – – – – – – r!

6. There is nothing sweeter than seeing l – – bs frisking in the fields.

7. Leopards love to lie along a l – – b of a tree and sleep.

8. The last four months of the year are called S – – – – – – – r, October, N – – – – – – r, D – – – – – – r.

Show your completed exercise to your teacher.

Unit 3

WORD ENDINGS -*ful*, -*ly*, -*ment*, -*tion*

1

There are a very large number of words which have -*ful* added to them. Here are some of them. Notice very carefully that there is only *one l* in *ful*.

beauti*ful*	wonder*ful*	aw*ful*
peace*ful*	cheer*ful*	success*ful*
though*tful*	use*ful*	grace*ful*

1. Write out this list of words in your exercise book.
2. Write the words out in your spelling dictionary.

EXERCISE 12

Make up sentences of your own, using the words which you are given below. Put these sentences in your exercise book.

1. beautiful   3. peaceful   5. useful   7. graceful
2. awful   4. thoughtful   6. successful 8. cheerful

> *Show your sentences to your teacher.*

2

When you add -*ly* to an adjective you form an *adverb*. The number of adverbs you make in this way is very large indeed. It is important that you know *how* to do this. Fortunately, the rules for adding -*ly* to a word are quite simple. With very few *exceptions*, you simply add -*ly* to the end of the word without *any* change to the first word. Here are some examples.

Adjective		Word Ending		Adverb
cruel	+	ly	=	cruelly
definite	+	ly	=	definitely

Nothing could be easier, could it?

60

EXERCISE 13

Write out in your exercise book, the adverbs *which are formed by adding* -ly *to the following adjectives.*

Adjective   +   ly   =   Adverb

1. exact
2. special
3. beautiful
4. sincere
5. dangerous

6. immediate
7. separate
8. quick
9. entire
10. cruel

Check with answers on page 141.

Note In a small number of words there is a change which takes place in the *adjective* when you add *-ly* to it. It is easy enough to *learn* these few words. Here are the most common words.

1. Adjectives which end in *y*, *e.g.* easy, busy. In these words you change the *y* to *i* before adding *-ly*, as you did on page 60.

busy	+	ly	=	busily
easy	+	ly	=	easily

2. Two words, *true* and *due*: when you add *-ly* to these words you drop the *e*.

true	+	ly	=	truly (no *e*)
due	+	ly	=	duly (no *e*)

3. In the words *gentle* and *probable*, the final *le* is dropped before a following *-ly*.

gentle	+	ly	=	gently
probable	+	ly	=	probably

1. *In your exercise book, write out the following list of* adverbs.

immediately	gently	sincerely	easily
probably	dangerously	separately	truly
beautifully	busily	extremely	definitely

2. *Now write these words into your spelling dictionary.*

3 You must know a large number of words which end in *-ment*. Here is a list of some which you may find useful in your writing.

argument	agreement	amusement
parliament	advertisement	equipment
government	excitement	entertainment

1. Write these words out in your exercise book.
2. Now write them out in your spelling dictionary.

Here are two exercises for you to do and then show to your teacher.

EXERCISE 14

Complete the following sentences in your own words. Write them out in your exercise book.

1. The two boys had an argument — .
2. The Houses of Parliament are — .
3. In the advertisement it said — .
4. We keep our equipment — .
5. The Government should — .

EXERCISE 15

Make up sentences of your own using the words from the following list. Write them out carefully in your exercise book.

1. excitement
2. amusement   entertainment
3. government   equipment
4. parliament   immediately
5. advertisement   argument

> *Show these exercises to your teacher.*

4

Here is a list of words ending in -*tion* which students sometimes find difficulty in spelling correctly.

addi*tion*	atten*tion*	collec*tion*
inven*tion*	recrea*tion*	irriga*tion*
ques*tion*	accommoda*tion*	condi*tion*

1. *Write out this list in your exercise book.*
2. *Now write these words into your spelling dictionary.*

Here are two exercises for you to do and then show to your teacher.

EXERCISE 16

Write out the following sentences in your exercise book, filling in the blanks from the list given above.

1. The junior class rushed into the r – – – – – – – – n hall.

2. My older sister is going to Peru later this year to give advice on
   i – – – – – – – – n so that they can grow better crops.

3. "This a – – – – – – – – – – – n is quite unsuitable," declared the fat man.

4. This was one q – – – – – – n which did not deserve an answer.

5. He said she could borrow the book on c – – – – – – – n that she returned it the next day.

EXERCISE 17

Finally, make up sentences of your own using the words from the list which follows and write them out in your exercise book.

1. addition   subtraction
2. question
3. accommodation   condition

4. collection   attention
5. invention   irrigation

Show these completed exercises to your teacher.

MODULE 6

Spelling Four

Unit 1

VOWEL CLUSTER — *ou*

This is one of the most common and, therefore, most important, combinations of letters in English. Because the list of words with *ou* in them is so large, we will deal with them in the following manner:

1. Words having *ou* in them
2. Words having *ough* in them
3. Words having *ought* in them
4. Words having *our* in them
5. Words having *ous* in them ⎱ We will deal with
6. Words having *ious* in them ⎰ these together.

Here is a list to learn of words containing *ou*.

wou ld	accou nt	cou ncil
dou ble	hou se	trou ble
wou nd	cou sin	thou sand

1. *Write these words out in your exercise book.*
2. *Write them out in your spelling dictionary.*

Here are two exercises for you to work through and then show to your teacher.

EXERCISE 1

Write the following sentences in your exercise book, filling in the blanks from the list given above.

1. He said that he w – – – d come home early, if he could.

2. The storekeeper sent his company's a – – – – – t in to the local
   c – – – – – l.

64

3. Whenever it rained, my father's old w – – – d gave him t – – – – – e.

4. My c – – – – n has the very same name as me.

5. For breakfast once I received an egg with a d – – – – e yolk.

6. My big sister said that there were thirty t – – – – – – d people at the hockey match, but I didn't believe her.

7. My mother asked me to pay her electricity a – – – – – t.

8. My brother is interested in politics and w – – – d like to be voted on to the c – – – – – l one day.

EXERCISE 2

Make up sentences of your own, using the words listed below and write them out in your exercise book.

1. cousin		3. troubled	wound	5. house	double
2. would	council	4. thousand	account		

> *Show these completed exercises to your teacher.*

Here is the list to learn of words containing *ough*.

although	cough	through
ploughed	enough	tough

1. *Write these words out in your exercise book.*
2. *Now write them out carefully into your spelling dictionary.*

Here are two exercises for you to work through and then show to your teacher.

EXERCISE 3

Write out the following sentences in your exercise book, filling in the blanks from the list given above.

1. A – – – – – – h my cousin was always getting into trouble, everybody liked him.

2. Every winter my grandmother develops a very bad c – – – h.

3. After the blizzard, we had to p – – – – h our way t – – – – – h the deep snow.

4. A turtle has an extremely t – – – h skin.

5. A – – – – – – h she tried hard, she simply couldn't climb to the top of the rope in the gym.

EXERCISE 4

Make up sentences of your own, using the words listed below. Write them out in your exercise book.

1. tough   enough   3. through   5. plough
2. although   enough   4. cough

> *Show these completed sentences to your teacher.*

3 Here is the list to learn of words containing *ought.*

> *bought   brought   thought   fought*

1. Write out these words in your exercise book.
2. Now write them in your spelling dictionary.

Here are two exercises for you to work through and then show to your teacher.

EXERCISE 5

Write out the following sentences in your exercise book, filling in the blanks from the list above.

1. Last year my uncle b – – – – t my sister, Tracy, a bicycle for her tenth birthday.

2. Once I t – – – – – t that I would like to be a teacher, now I'm not so sure!

3. The sales assistant b – – – – – t me a pair of gloves from the stock room.

4. Benny's cousin once f – – – – t for the World Boxing Championship.

5. When my brother was sick last year, he t – – – – – t that he saw snakes crawling along the ceiling!

EXERCISE 6

Make up sentences of your own, using the words listed below.

1. thought	3. bought	thousand	5. fought
2. would	4. brought	coloured	

> Show these completed exercises to your teacher.

Here is the list to learn of words containing *our*.

flour	*neighbour*	*behaviour*	*favourite*
honour	*courage*	*fourth*	*colour*

1. *Write out these words in your exercise book.*
2. *Now write them out in your spelling dictionary.*

Here are two exercises for you to work through and then show to your teacher.

EXERCISE 7

Write out the following sentences in your exercise book filling in the blanks from the list above.

1. Our n – – – – – – – r is always borrowing f – – – r or salt or sugar from my mother.

2. Because of her c – – – – – e in overcoming her handicap, my friend, Jill, was a great f – – – – – – – e with everyone in the class.

3. What c – – – – r are your eyes?

4. When you are addressing a judge, you call him, Your H – – – – r.

5. "This is the third or f – – – – h time you have been brought before me," said the Headteacher. "Next time, you will find yourself in real trouble."

EXERCISE 8

Make up sentences of your own, using the words listed below and write them out in your exercise book.

1. neighbour
2. courageous   fourth
3. favourites
4. behaviour
5. colouring

Show your completed sentences to your teacher.

Here are lists to learn of words containing *ous* and *ious*.

fam*ous*	jeal*ous*	numer*ous*
enorm*ous*	relig*ious*	anx*ious*
deli*cious*	myster*ious*	cur*ious*

1. *Write out these sentences in your exercise book.*
2. *Now write them out in your spelling dictionary.*

Here are two exercises for you to work through and then show to your teacher.

EXERCISE 9

Write out the following sentences in your exercise book, filling in the blanks from the list given above.

1. He said that the rock-cakes had been quite d – – – – – – – s.

2. I often think it would be wonderful to be really f – – – – s.

3. The sword on the wall was marked with c – – – – – s carvings. It looked very m – – – – – – – – s.

4. As I waited for the bus, I began to feel a – – – – – s.

5. My mother is a deeply r – – – – – – – s person and goes to church every week.

EXERCISE 10

Make up sentences of your own, using the words listed below. Write them out in your exercise book.

1. jealous
2. curious
3. delicious
4. mysterious
5. numerous   enormous

> *Show these exercises to your teacher.*
> *Correct any spelling mistakes you have made recently in your class writing and add the words to your spelling dictionary.*

Unit 2

VOWEL CLUSTER – *au*

Here is a list of the commonest words containing the vowel cluster *au*.

*au*nt	*Au*gust	bec*au*se
s*au*cepan	s*au*cer	s*au*sage
bea*u*ty	*au*dience	l*au*ghed

1. *Write out these words in your exercise book.*
2. *Now write them out* carefully *in your spelling dictionary.*

Here are two exercises for you to work through and then show to your teacher.

EXERCISE 11

Write out the following sentences in your exercise book, filling in the blanks from the list given above.

1. My a – – t was considered a great b – – – – y when she was a young woman.

2. It is in the kitchen that you would expect to find a s – – – – – e, a s – – – – – – n and a s – – – – r.

3. The a – – – – – – e l – – – – – d when the comic slipped and fell.

4. A – – – – t is usually a warm month in this part of the country.

5. B – – – – – e l broke my leg, I had to spend several months in plaster.

69

EXERCISE 12

Make up sentences of your own, using the words given below, in your exercise book.

1. saucepan
2. because   laughed
3. aunt   audience
4. saucer   sausage
5. beauty   August

> *Show these exercises to your teacher.*

2 Here is a list of words containing *aught* which you should learn.

> *taught*   *caught*   *laughter*   *naughty*   *daughter*

1. *Write out these words in your exercise book.*
2. *Now write out the words again in your spelling dictionary, taking care to put them into the proper place.*

Here are two exercises for you to work through and then show to your teacher.

EXERCISE 13

Write out the following sentences in your exercise book, filling in the blanks from the list above.

1. The teacher who t – – – – t my d – – – – – – r said that she had been very n – – – – – y.
2. My aunt c – – – – t the ten o'clock train.
3. Last A – – – – t, my father t – – – – t me to swim.
4. They say that l – – – – – – r makes the world go round.
5. Because the weather was bad last autumn, my d – – – – – – r c – – – – t a nasty cold.

70

EXERCISE 14

Make up sentences of your own in your exercise book, using the list of words below.

1. aunt   taught
2. daughter   saucepan
3. caught   saucer
4. naughty
5. daughter   beautiful

> *Show these exercises to your teacher.*

CONSONANT CLUSTERS *-ght, kn*

1

As you will already have seen from the previous exercises, the combination *ght* occurs in a large number of words which we all use frequently. Let us practise *some* of them.

delighted	bright	fright
sight	thought	bought
straight	height	weight

1. *Write these words out in your exercise book.*
2. *Now write them out in the proper place in your spelling dictionary.*

Here are two exercises for you to work through and then show to your teacher.

EXERCISE 15

Write out the following sentences in your exercise book, filling in the blanks from the list given above.

1. Frank brought back the book which I b – – – – t that morning.

2. She told me angrily that I had no right giving her a f – – – – t like that.

3. The recruiting officer asked my h – – – – t and w – – – – t.

4. He suddenly saw a b – – – – t light appearing s – – – – – – t ahead.

5. Because it was so warm, I t – – – – – t that I would go for a swim.

71

EXERCISE 16

Make up sentences of your own using words in the list below.

1. straight
2. height   weight
3. bought
4. delighted
5. taught

> *Show these completed sentences to your teacher.*

Here is a list of words containing *kn* which you should take special care with in your written work.

*kn*ow	*kn*ife	*kn*ew	*kn*ight
*kn*itting	*kn*ee	*kn*owledge	un*kn*own

1. *Write out these words in your exercise book.*
2. *Now write them out again in your spelling dictionary.*

Here are two exercises for you to work through and then show to your teacher.

EXERCISE 17

Write out the following sentences in your exercise book, filling in the blanks from the list given above.

1. "Do you k – – w anything about k – – – – – g?" asked the old woman.

2. The k – – – – t had a k – – – e strapped to his thigh as well as a sword.

3. Last August, I visited the tomb of the U – – – – – n Warrior.

4. Peter won the General K – – – – – – – e prize.

5. Isn't it funny that you never pronounce the 'k' in words like 'k – – e', 'k – – – e', 'k – – – – – – – e,' and 'u – – – – – n'?

EXERCISE 18

Make up sentences of your own in your exercise book, using the words given below.

1. know   laughter
2. knowledge   knitting
3. unknown   fought
4. knitting   needle
5. knight   laughed

> *Show these completed exercises to your teacher.*

Unit 3

WORD ENDINGS *-ance, -ence, -able, -ible*

Here is a list of common words which end with *-ance*.

dist*ance*	bal*ance*	appear*ance*
d*ance*	acquaint*ance*	import*ance*
	nuis*ance*	

1. *Write out these words in your exercise book.*
2. *Now write them out again in your spelling dictionary.*

Here are two exercises for you to work through and then show to your teacher.

EXERCISE 19

Write out the following sentences in your exercise book, filling in the blanks from the list given above.

1. At the half way d – – – – – – e one of the runners fell out of the race with exhaustion.

2. It is a n – – – – – – e to have to carry an umbrella when it doesn't rain.

3. The audience did not like the speaker, because he was full of his own i – – – – – – – – e.

4. Everybody thought that the player had made a very good first a – – – – – – – – e.

5. Keeping your b – – – – – e is very important, if you are an ice-skater.

EXERCISE 20

Make up sentences of your own in your exercise book, using the words given below.

1. importance
2. dance
3. appearance
4. nuisance
5. acquaintance

Show these completed exercises to your teacher.

Here is an important list of words which you should learn ending in -*ence*.

ab*sence*	differ*ence*	sen*tence*
aud*ience*	exper*ience*	intellig*ence*

1. *Write out these words in your exercise book.*
2. *Now write them out again in your spelling dictionary.*

Here are two exercises for you to work through and then show to your teacher.

EXERCISE 21

Write out the following sentences in your exercise book, filling in the blanks from the list given above.

1. After an a – – – – – e of several weeks, the missing explorer staggered out of the jungle.

2. The d – – – – – – – e between one pea and another is very hard to tell.

3. Last night I had a dreadful e – – – – – – – e while driving home from work.

4. Everyone admired him because of his i – – – – – – – – – e.

5. The judge gave Light-Fingers Brady a long prison s – – – – – – e.

EXERCISE 22

Make up your own sentences and write them out in your exercise book, using the words in the list given below.

1. absences
2. experiences   difference
3. sentences
4. intelligence   audience
5. difference

> Show these completed exercises to your teacher.

3

The endings *-able* and *-ible* are often confused. This section will help you to learn the difference between them. First, learn this list ending in *-able*.

laugh*able*	comfort*able*	valu*able*	excit*able*
prob*able*	notice*able*	change*able*	knowledge*able*

1. Write out these words in your exercise book.
2. Now write out these words carefully in your spelling dictionary.

Here are four exercises for you to work through and then show to your teacher.

EXERCISE 23

Write out the following sentences in your exercise book, filling in the blanks from the words given above.

1. Mary found the armchair very c – – – – – – – – – e and promptly fell asleep.

2. It is p – – – – – – e that it will rain at least ten times in April.

3. After two days in hospital, there was a n – – – – – – – – e improvement in my grandfather's condition.

4. My mother always says that my big sister is as c – – – – – – – – e as the weather.

5. The clock which I found in the rubbish bin turned out to be very v – – – – – – e.

EXERCISE 24

Make up sentences of your own in your exercise book, using the words given in the list below.

1. excitable   laughter
2. probable   August
3. laughable
4. knowledgeable
5. comfortable

Here is the list which ends with *-ible*.

possible terrible forcible impossible horrible

1. *Write out these words in your exercise book.*
2. *Now write them out again in your spelling dictionary.*

EXERCISE 25

Write out the following sentences in your exercise book, filling in the blanks from the list given above.

1. It is now p – – – – – – e for man to go to the moon.

2. There was a t – – – – – – e crash outside our home last night.

3. The policeman said that the crook had made a f – – – – – – e entrance.

4. It is i – – – – – – – – e to read in a noisy room.

5. "Oh, that tastes h – – – – – – e!" spluttered my young brother when the doctor tried to give him his medicine.

EXERCISE 26

In this final exercise, make up sentences of your own in your exercise book, using the words given below.

1. possible
2. impossible   saucer
3. terrible   experience
4. horrible   sight
5. possible   caught

Show these four exercises to your teacher.

The Comma

There are *two* main uses of the *comma*:

1. To *separate* items in a list. (Unit 1)
2. To *mark off* parts of a sentence. (Units 2 & 3)

Unit 1 Items in a List
Unit Test

Write out the following sentences, putting in the missing commas.

1. Sammy put his trunks towel goggles and flippers into the locker.
2. The clinic will open on Mondays Tuesdays Thursdays and Saturday morning.
3. The stranger was a tall lean weather-beaten man.
4. My car needed a new exhaust gearbox radiator and two front tyres.
5. Spacious top-flat containing living-room kitchen two bedrooms bathroom.
6. We joined Mr Bromley John and Mary Bennett the Smith twins and Deirdre at the airport.

> Check with the answers on page 142.
> If you made no mistakes, go to Unit 2 on page 80.
> If you made any mistakes, continue with this unit.

Example 1 Joe's dog has two ears, a tail, a nose and a very bad temper.

Notice that when the list of items finishes with *and* you *do not* put a *comma* before or after the word *and*.

Example 2 For Christmas the boy was given a football strip, a pair of boots, a track-suit and a leather football.

No Comma Here

EXERCISE 1

Copy out in your exercise book the following sentences adding the information which is contained in the pictures. Commas are needed in each sentence.

1. For her birthday the little girl was given — .

2. On the television show the old age pensioner won — .

3. A bicycle is made up of — .

4. Standing at the bus-stop were — .

5. Among the animals and birds we saw at the wild life park were — .

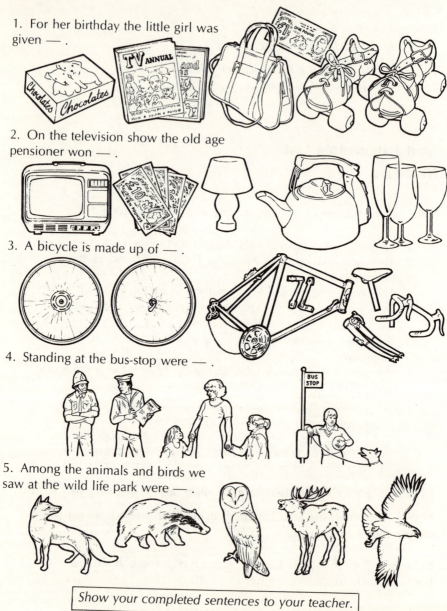

Show your completed sentences to your teacher.

EXERCISE 2

Write out the following sentences in your exercise book, putting in the commas correctly.

1. The king's daughter was selfish vain and very unhappy.
2. My favourite breakfast is bacon eggs toast and a large mug of steaming hot tea.
3. My mother asked me to go to the shops and buy a paper a box of matches two bars of chocolate and a battery for the transistor.
4. The ground floor flat comprises living room three bedrooms kitchen and bathroom.
5. There was a shortage of carrots Brussels sprouts cabbages and potatoes because of the recent severe frost.
6. Susan came fourth in the high jump second in the long jump third in the javelin and beat all the boys in the shot putt.
7. When asked to empty his pockets by the teacher, the wee boy produced two packets of bubble-gum a rusty pen-knife four sticks of chalk and the remains of a smoked sausage.
8. On the seventh day of Christmas my true-love gave to me seven swans a-swimming six geese a-laying five gold rings four calling birds three French hens two turtle doves and a partridge in a pear tree.

Check with the answers on page 142.

EXERCISE 3

"I packed my bag and in it I put . . . ." You have probably played this game. You will remember that you add another item when it is your turn. The game is much funnier if you add unusual items. In your exercise book, write out the six sentences as shown below, completing them by adding One Item each time. Remember the commas.

1. I packed my bag and in it I put . . . (1 item)
2. I packed my bag and in it I put . . . (2 items)
3. I packed my bag and in it I put . . . (3 items)
4. I packed my bag and in it I put . . . (4 items)
5. I packed my bag and in it I put . . . (5 items)
6. I packed my bag and in it I put . . . (6 items)

You should now have a long list, separated by commas.

Show your completed sentences to your teacher.

Unit 2 Commas used to mark off part of a sentence

Unit Test

Write out these sentences putting in the missing commas.

1. I asked Tommy the boy next-door if he had seen our cat.
2. What you should do of course is to phone for the police.
3. The nurse who had just come on duty gave me a drink of water.
4. Mr Wong the restaurant owner showed us to a table near the window.
5. The burst pipe which had thawed out overnight ruined the bedroom ceiling.
6. The world heavy-weight champion aged thirty-eight retained his title in New York.

> Check with the answers on page 143.
> If you made no mistakes, go to Unit 3 on page 83.
> If you made any mistakes, continue with this unit.

Here is a good sentence:

Pedro seized the lion in a grip of iron.

This sentence has something *definite* to say and says it *directly*. When you write sentences of your own you should try to make them as *direct* and *clear* as possible.

   Commas help you to write sentences *clearly*. *Imagine* that a sentence is like a section of railway line.

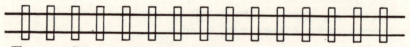

The most *direct route* between *two* stations would be a *straight line*.

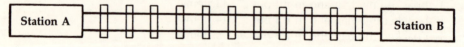

Pedro seized the lion in a grip of iron.

Sometimes, you might want to *add* something to a sentence like this. For example, you might want to say that Pedro was the Strongman's son or that he had only one leg!

Now these things are not so *important* as the fact that he tackled the lion, but they are still *interesting*.

If you think of the *sentence* as part of a railway line, it is like leaving the *main line* and going into a *siding* before coming back to the *main line*.

Here is what it might look like in a diagram.

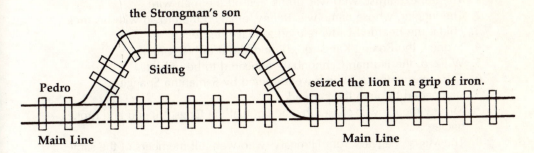

To leave the main railway line and go into a siding you would switch by using *points*.

At the place where your sentence leaves the main line and comes back again you put *commas*.

The commas act like points on a railway line. This *clearly* marks off the less important detail from the main part of the sentence. Here is what the sentence looks like in the form of a diagram.

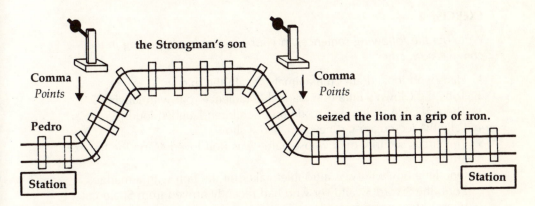

And here is what it looks like written as a sentence.

Pedro, the Strongman's son, seized the lion in a grip of iron.

Here is another example.

Mr Spangler, the Ringmaster, introduced the Boxing Kangaroo.

EXERCISE 1

Place your exercise book sideways *and draw some railway type diagrams for the following sentences.*
Write the words above the line as in the examples on page 81.

1. The trapeze artist, who was drunk, fell off the high wire.
2. The juggler, whose name was Benny, amazed the crowd with his tricks.
3. Hilda, the Bearded Lady, refused to leave her tent.
4. Sydney, the Boxing Kangaroo, bounded out of his corner.
5. Whizzo, the Human Cannonball, appeared to be unhurt.
6. The Liberty Horses, which were trained by Samantha Spangler, stampeded through the car park.
7. Mickey the Clown, chased by the Footballing Dogs, tripped and broke his leg.
8. The Merry Magyars from Hungary, who were all members of the same family, opened the second half of the programme.

> *Show your completed work to your teacher.*

EXERCISE 2

Write out the following sentences in your exercise book, putting in the commas correctly.

1. Hans who looked after the animals caught the thieves.
2. Toby the Clown's little dog made the audience roar with laughter.
3. The audience which was made up of children laughed loudly.
4. Sally the ice-cream girl never missed a show.
5. The circus security man whose name was Rolf loved Maria the trapeze artiste.
6. One little boy who was a trouble-maker hit the lion with a marble.
7. Zorro the Sword Swallower who had recently arrived from Spain cut himself shaving and could not appear that afternoon.
8. Mr Spangler who was also one of the clowns hurriedly changed into a pair of baggy trousers and a ragged shirt.

> *Check with the answers on page 143.*

Unit 3 Joining sentences

Unit Test

Write out these sentences, putting in the missing commas.

1. My sister apologised to me but I know she didn't mean it.
2. A comma is used to separate items in a list as shown in Unit 1.
3. It will be generally dull and cloudy tomorrow though temperatures will be above average for the time of the year.
4. The trapper decided to press on to Red River Falls which was twenty miles farther north.
5. When the exam finished the teacher told us to put our pens away and leave the room quietly.
6. The rescue team set off up the mountain although they knew there was little chance of finding any survivors.

Check with the answers on page 143.
If you made no mistakes, go to the Supplementary Exercises on page 86.
If you made any mistakes, continue with this unit.

Sometimes, sentences contain *two* different ideas which are *complete* and can stand by themselves.

Here are two sentences.

Mary washed her hair.   She came downstairs.

You could, however, *join* these *two* ideas into *one* sentence. For example, you might want to make it clear that Mary came downstairs *after* she had washed her hair. You do this by using a *joining word*, or *conjunction*, plus a *comma*.

Mary came downstairs, after she washed her hair.

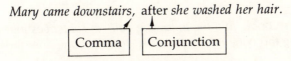

You could write this sentence another way.

After she washed her hair, Mary came downstairs.

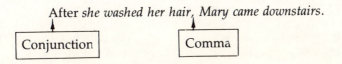

On the other hand, you might want to say that Mary washed her hair *after* she came downstairs and not *before*. You do this in the same way.

After *Mary came downstairs, she washed her hair.*

OR

Mary washed her hair, after *she came downstairs.*

EXERCISE 1

Use the same two sentences:

Mary washed her hair. She came downstairs

Join them together into one sentence, using the conjunction before *plus a comma. If you switch them around, you should be able to write* four *sentences, as in the examples above.*

> *Check with the answers on page 144.*

This is how you deal with all *joining words*, or *conjunctions*. You use them with a *comma* to mark off part of the sentence.

Here are some of the commonest *conjunctions*.

although	though	and	but	when	after	before
as	as soon as	while	since	because	until	

EXERCISE 2

In your exercise book, join the following pairs of sentences into one sentence using the conjunction which is shown. Remember the commas!

Example

Two Sentences	Conjunction	Joined Sentence
The little boy laughed. His pal tickled him.	*when*	The little boy laughed, when his pal tickled him.

1. The little girl laughed. Her pal slipped on a banana skin.   *when*   ?

2. I have been trying to help you. You do not realise it.   *although*   ?

3. John did what he was told. Peter did not pay any attention.   *but*   ?

4. The game was cancelled. The pitch was waterlogged.   *as*   ?

5. You should not swim after a heavy meal. You might develop stomach cramp.   *because*   ?

6. Several passengers received minor injuries. It was a miracle that no one was killed.   *although*   ?

7. The circus performer used to dive ten metres into a wet sponge. One day he broke his neck.   *until*   ?

8. He broke his neck. Someone had wrung out the sponge!   *because*   ?

Check with the answers on page 144.

EXERCISE 3

Write out the following sentences in your exercise book, filling in the blanks with your own words to complete the sentences.

1. When you go swimming, — .
2. He was a good runner, though — .
3. If you want to make a hit record, — .
4. When I am older, — .
5. Don't watch this programme, if — .
6. — , but I can't afford to buy one.
7. Unless you are a Scotsman, — .
8. — , when you see flames.
9. I'm not saying his feet are big, but — .
10. — , whoever you are!

> *Show your completed sentences to your teacher.*

SUPPLEMENTARY EXERCISES

EXERCISE A

Below is a copy of a recent Government notice which gives sensible advice on FIRE PREVENTION. All the commas have been removed. Your task is to rewrite this notice in your exercise book putting in all the commas. You may also learn ways of avoiding fires in your home!

Children

Do keep matches lighters cigarettes out of their reach. Do not ever leave them alone in the home. Do guard all fires radiators and stoves and ensure that all heaters and electric fires are in good order. Do keep flammable liquids such as petrol paraffin white spirit and methylated spirits outdoors in proper containers and take care not to use paints or adhesives near a naked flame. Do not store combustibles such as newspapers rags and boxes especially under the stairs in the attic or in similar places.

Before going to bed

Do switch off and unplug the TV set and all other appliances not in use settle down coal or coke fires checking that the fire guard is in position and check that no cigarette ends are still burning. Do not forget after making these checks to close all doors and windows.

> *Check with the answers on page 144.*

EXERCISE B

Write out the following sentences in your exercise book, putting in the commas which have been missed out. If you can complete these final examples successfully, you should be able to use the comma correctly in your own writing.

1. Something appeared not to the sides or behind but almost directly in front of him. It was bright and moving incredibly fast and then it was firing just above him. Taken completely by surprise the Imperial fighter came apart just as the pilot realised what had happened.

   (from *Star Wars* by George Lucas)

2. Smith's room was small and oddly shaped owing to its situation under the roof. It was as though the builder arriving nearly at the summit of his labour had come upon this extra space by surprise and on the spur of the moment had popped a door and window to it so's not to embarrass the stairs with leading to nowhere. A bed a chest and a chair were the sole furnishings – and a pot of strong sweet herbs. For though Miss Mansfield could burn the sheets after Smith had slept in them she could not burn the room so the herbs were the next best thing.

   (from *Smith* by Leon Garfield)

3. Start cooking with gas and you've never felt so in command of things. That quick clean obedient blue flame changes from the slightest simmer to fierce heat at the turn of your fingers. And because it's so easy to control gas it's easy to control your fuel bill too! Speedy economical gas.

   (*British Gas publicity*)

> *Check with the answers on page 145.*

MODULE 8

The Paragraph

Unit 1

INTRODUCTION

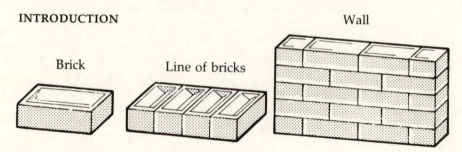

Brick   Line of bricks   Wall

Just as in building, *bricks* can be made into *lines of bricks* and then into *walls of bricks*, so *Words* can be made into *Sentences*, and *Sentences* into *Paragraphs*.

Here is an example.

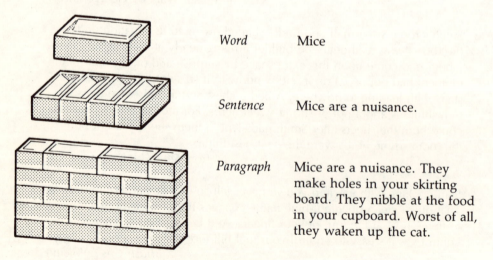

Word   Mice

Sentence   Mice are a nuisance.

Paragraph   Mice are a nuisance. They make holes in your skirting board. They nibble at the food in your cupboard. Worst of all, they waken up the cat.

Notice, in the *paragraph* above, the first *sentence* tells you that mice are a nuisance. The other three sentences tell you *why* they are a nuisance. This is a very simple kind of paragraph.

EXERCISE 1

Copy out the following examples in your exercise book and complete the paragraphs by adding two or three more sentences. Try, as usual, to make your writing interesting.

1.

	Word	Rain
	Sentence	Rain is horrible.
	Paragraph	Rain is horrible. It . . .

2.

	Word	Cars
	Sentence	Cars are noisy.
	Paragraph	Cars are noisy. They . . .

3.

	Word	Summer
	Sentence	Summer is the best season of the year.
	Paragraph	Summer is the best season of the year. Summer . . .

4.

	Word	Winter
	Sentence	Winter can be fun.
	Paragraph	Winter can be fun. In winter you . . .

5.

	Word	Television
	Sentence	Television plays an important part in our lives.
	Paragraph	Television plays an important part in our lives. Without television we . . .

Show your work to your teacher. If you have managed to do the exercise properly, you can actually write in paragraphs.

WHY HAVE PARAGRAPHS?

Quite simply we have paragraphs so that the reader can easily follow what we are saying. If we didn't split up our writing into *sections*, it would be very difficult to read and understand.

Here is an example
The following simple recipe is written out in two ways, one *without* paragraphs and one *with* paragraphs. Which is the easiest to read? Which one could you follow more easily, if you were making the meal?

Without Paragraphs

3 or 4 eggs; seasoning; 1–2 tablespoons milk or thin cream; 25 g margarine or butter. Beat the eggs with seasoning and the milk or cream. It is not *essential* to add milk or cream, although this gives a lighter scrambled egg. Melt the margarine or butter in a saucepan. Add the eggs, make sure the heat is low, then leave the eggs for about one minute. Stir gently with a wooden spoon until lightly set. Spoon on to hot buttered toast or fried bread. Scrambled eggs make a lovely light meal served with piped creamed potatoes.

With Paragraphs

3 or 4 eggs; seasoning; 1–2 tablespoons milk or thin cream; 25 g margarine or butter.

Beat the eggs with seasoning and the milk or cream. It is not *essential* to add milk or cream, although this gives a lighter scrambled egg.

Melt the margarine or butter in a saucepan. Add the eggs, make sure the heat is low then leave the eggs for about one minute. Stir gently with a wooden spoon until lightly set.

Spoon on to hot buttered toast or fried bread. Scrambled eggs make a light meal served with piped creamed potatoes.

Obviously, it is easier to follow a recipe when it is set out in *sections*. When it is set out in *paragraphs*, you can see the *plan* of the piece of writing.

Here is the *plan* of the recipe for Scrambled Eggs which you were given.

Paragraph 1 The ingredients
Paragraph 2 Mixing the ingredients together
Paragraph 3 Cooking the ingredients
Paragraph 4 Serving the meal

EXERCISE 2

Now try this for yourself. In the following exercise you are given a recipe without any paragraphs. Then you are given the plan of the recipe. What you must do is to write out the recipe, in your exercise book, in paragraphs the way it would appear in a newspaper or magazine.

Without Paragraphs

Apple Fritters
100 g self-raising flour; 1 standard egg, separated; about 125 ml tepid water; 1 very large cooking apple; lard or corn oil for deep frying; 30 g caster sugar, optional. Sift the flour into a mixing bowl; make a hollow in the centre of the flour and add the egg yolk. Gradually add tepid water until you have a thick mixture (it should be stiff enough to coat the back of a wooden spoon). Peel and core apple carefully. Cut into 8 thin rings. Gently heat the pan of lard or oil. Whisk egg white until very stiff and snowy then fold into the batter. Dip the apple slices into the batter and deep fry in hot oil, 4 at a time, for about 2 minutes, or until they are puffed up and golden. Drain on absorbent kitchen paper. If you're using sugar, sprinkle it on the fritters and serve.

The ingredients

Making the mix

Preparing the apple

Cooking the ingredients

Serving the fritters

> *Now check your answer with page 146. If you made any mistakes in writing out the paragraphs, copy out the recipe correctly in your exercise book.*

EXERCISE 3

Each of us has a favourite sandwich. Sometimes these favourite sandwiches are ones which other people think are very strange. Some people, for example, like treacle and chutney in a sandwich. Some others like cold fish-fingers in their sandwich! Then there is peanut butter and jam! Write out in your exercise book – as if it were a recipe – how it is you make your favourite sandwich.

Put the name of your sandwich at the top of the page.

Paragraph One	The ingredients
Paragraph Two	How you put it together.
	(Is it toasted, for example?)
Paragraph Three	How you serve it.

> *When you have finished this exercise, show it to your teacher.*

But it isn't *only* in recipes that you have to do things in order, giving a *paragraph* to each section of the work or task. If you were writing out instructions on how to wrap up a parcel or how to play a game, you would also set it out in *paragraphs* to make it easier to follow the stages.

EXERCISE 4

In your exercise book, write a series of short paragraphs *on the two examples given below.*

A. Washing the Dishes

Plan
1. Collecting the dishes.
   (How do you stack them?)
2. Preparing the water.
   (Note the temperature and the washing up liquid.)
3. In which order do you wash them?
4. Standing them to dry.
   (Have you any tips to offer?)
5. Putting them back in the cupboard.

B. Wiring a Plug

Plan

1. The tools you might need.
2. Unscrewing the plug.
   (How many screws do you have to unscrew?)
3. Attaching the wires.
   (Make sure you put the wires in the right place!)
4. Screwing the plug back together again.

> *Show these two exercises to your teacher.*

E = Earth (green & yellow)

L = Live (brown)

N = Neutral (blue)

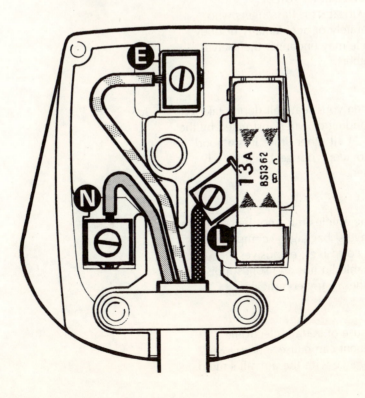

PLANNING PARAGRAPHS

EXERCISE 5

In this exercise you are given four passages containing a number of paragraphs set out in the proper way. Write out the plan of each passage in your exercise book. Part of the first one is given to help you.

PARAGRAPHS

A. Safety in Aeroplanes

By following the instructions given by the crew of the aircraft, you will be contributing to flight safety.

Smoking is not allowed during take-off, or at any time as directed by the pilot. SMOKING IS NOT ALLOWED AT ANY TIME IN TOILET COMPARTMENTS. Passengers who deliberately or accidentally disobey this rule may endanger themselves and others.

Fasten your seat belt during take-off and landing or when instructed by the crew. At all other times it is a good idea to keep your seat belt loosely fastened.

Some articles must not be carried in passengers' baggage – compressed gases, corrosives, explosives, flammable liquids and solids, poisons and other restricted articles.

The use of certain electronic equipment can cause serious interference with the aircraft's radio

PLAN

Safety in Aeroplanes

1. Why we must follow safety instructions

2. When you may not smoke

3. ?

4. ?

5. ?

94

navigation equipment. Do not switch on portable radios, transmitters or television sets on board the aircraft. But portable recorders, hearing aids and heart pacemakers may be used on board.

> *Show this exercise to your teacher.*
> *Now try the next three examples in the same way.*
> *Remember to write one sentence for each paragraph.*

B. Pests and Diseases of House Plants

Healthy plants are more resistant to pests and diseases than neglected ones, but it is worth knowing something about the various treatments.

Ants are a nuisance in the home, although they do not actually damage plants. They loosen the soil and carry diseases from one plant to another. They can be removed with ant killer.

Aphids (greenfly), whitefly, blackfly and red spider mites attack the undersides of leaves and young shoots. They can be controlled with special sprays, which are quite safe to use indoors.

Mealy bugs are found on the stems and stem joints of house plants. They can be sprayed or removed by rubbing with a cotton bud soaked in methylated spirits.

Mildew is generally the result of overwatering or overcrowding the plants. Improve the ventilation of affected plants, and avoid overwatering.

Rust is another disease which attacks many plants. It should be treated with a weed-killer after removing the dead leaves.

> *Show your completed paragraph plan to your teacher.*

C. The Al Abu Holiday Apartments

If you want to be right at the centre of the action, then the situation of the Al Abu Apartments could hardly be bettered.

Here you are surrounded by shops, bars, cafes. Right below you is a splendid restaurant tempting you with many fascinating dishes as well as a much appreciated bacon and eggs breakfast, if you wish.

The two bedrooms, one with twin beds, adjoin the delightful living room and look on to the big balcony, while the dining space can seat five for meals and the kitchen is well laid-out for speedy catering. The bathroom features bath, shower, wc, mirror and 200 volt shaving point.

Although you are in a quiet situation, the area abounds with town attractions and the beach is a mere sandal stroll away!

> *Show your completed paragraph plan to your teacher.*

D. Denver – USA

One should try to get to Denver whatever the excuse – business trip, family reunion, holiday, or just to escape the law!

A holiday in Colorado used to be expensive. It is not now. A good class hotel in a quiet neighbourhood would cost no more than £8 to £9.50 per person per day.

This charge covers accommodation in a spacious double room with fitted carpets, modern furniture, air conditioning and, if you have a front room, a marvellous view of the Rocky Mountains!

Obviously, any newcomer to Denver wants to see the Rocky Mountains. The parts nearest the town are not only the most developed but also the most beautiful. The more rugged areas with some of the well-known winter sports centres lie further west.

Roads in the Rockies are good, although they climb to over 4200 metres. Also the mountains have mostly gentle slopes without steep gradients. Actually the traveller is surprised to see long stretches of flat land between ranges. Locally they are called 'parks'.

A tour of the Rockies need not be longer than some 800 kilometres. It can also be broken down into a series of day trips based on Denver itself.

> *Show your completed paragraph plan to your teacher.*

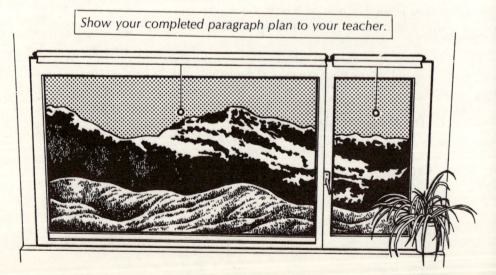

SETTING OUT PARAGRAPHS

It is important that you should be able to set out your *paragraphs* neatly on the page. Writing always looks much better when it is properly set out. Fortunately, the rules for setting out paragraphs are quite *simple*.

The illustration shows how your *paragraphs* should be spaced out. When you are doing the exercises which follow, you can refer back to it.

When writing in any book or paper which has *LINES* and a *MARGIN*:

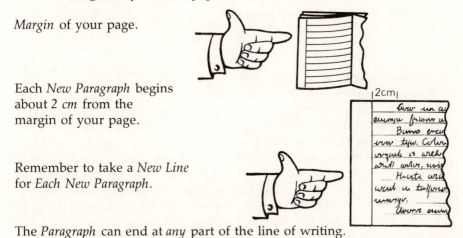

Margin of your page.

Each *New Paragraph* begins about *2 cm* from the margin of your page.

Remember to take a *New Line* for *Each New Paragraph*.

The *Paragraph* can end at *any* part of the line of writing.

EXERCISE 6

Write out the following two passages in paragraphs in your exercise book. You are told before each passage, how many paragraphs you should have. To help you one of the paragraphs in each passage has been underlined.

A. Holbein Holiday Apartments

(There are five paragraphs in this passage.)

The Holbein Holiday Apartments are ideally situated in the principal hotel area of San Antonio, and that's an open invitation to explore the many dances and entertainments which make this resort one of the happiest holiday spots under the sun. Each apartment contains 2 bedrooms separated by a splendidly styled bathroom. The living/dining area is a clever blend of rich dark woods and complementary coloured tiles, tastefully furnished, to suit 5 guests (an extra bed can be accommodated in the living area). The 15 minute walk to town takes you past an interesting variety of hotels, traditional homes and bars while the beach is only 600 metres away. Kitchen fittings and equipment are ultra-modern for ease and efficiency including cooker, grill, fridge, pots, pans, cutlery, china, etc. The balcony is spacious and if you can forego its natural sunny attractions, all the facilities of the popular and lively Hotel Putchet are directly over the road – and the swimming pool is a challenge in itself.

> Check with the answers on page 146. If you have made any mistakes, copy the passage out correctly in your exercise book.

B. Salmon Fishing

(*There are* four paragraphs *in this passage*)

By this time, I had seen more than enough of salmon nets, but we were not finished with them yet. The dirty bag net Big Willie and I had been working on before dinner had to be lifted from the river bank, and spread on the grass of the drying green. I realised then that the sea was the master of the salmon fishing. As fast as we cleaned and dried the nets, we had to start packing the day's catch in ice, for the boat from Portree called for the fish every Wednesday and Saturday. Back and forwards we plodded, between the store shed and the river, lugging the heavy fish boxes aboard the coble. We were taking the last two boxes down when Long John called that the boat was coming. She was barely in sight, no more than a small speck in the south, but by the time we had put out in the coble, I was able to make out her covered wheelhouse. She was a converted fishing boat, well suited for the job of transporting the salmon to Portree.

(*Master of Morgana* by Allan Campbell McLean)

> Check with the answers on page 147. If you have made any mistakes copy the passage out correctly in your exercise book.

EXERCISE 7 (a)

In your exercise book, write out the following passage in paragraphs. There are four paragraphs in this passage. To help you, one paragraph has been underlined.

Ali Baba was a poor woodcutter, who lived in a small town in Persia very many years ago and who earned his living by selling his wood in the market-place. One day as he was riding his mule through the forest on his way home, he saw an enormous cloud of dust which seemed to be moving towards him. As it got nearer it turned out to be a troop of horsemen, so Ali Baba got off his mule and climbed up into a tree to hide, fearing they might be robbers. Robbers they were indeed, forty of them, and they rode past the tree where Ali was hiding, alighted from their horses outside a huge rock, and removed their saddle-bags which seemed to be very heavy. Then Ali Baba heard the man at the head of the troop (apparently the leader) call out in a loud voice the words, "Open Sesame!" and to his great astonishment, a huge door in the rock opened slowly and all forty robbers went inside carrying their loaded saddle-bags.

> Check with the answers on page 147. If you made any mistakes, copy the passage out correctly in your exercise book.

EXERCISE 7 (b)

In your exercise book, write four or five (or more if you like) paragraphs describing what happens next in the Ali Baba story. Pick up the story from the moment when Ali Baba himself goes up to the rock and says the magic words, "Open Sesame!"

> Show your story to your teacher.

Unit 2 Letter writing

INTRODUCTION

At some time in our lives all of us are going to write someone a *letter*. It might be a letter of application for a job, or a letter of complaint, or a letter to the tax-man. It might be a letter to the school about your son or daughter. It might be a letter to a friend or another member of your family.

All of these letters will look better if they have proper *paragraphs*. They will also be much easier to read. *Writing a letter is an important skill. It is also quite easy.*

Let us practise writing a few letters and, at the same time, learn more about the art of writing *paragraphs*.

There are two skills involved in writing a letter. First, we must make sure that the letter is set out properly on the paper. We will call this the *lay-out* of the letter.

Secondly, we must state our message, or information, as clearly as possible. We will call this the *content* of the letter.

> *Lay-out* = What the letter looks like
> *Content* = What the letter says

The rules about setting out a letter are quite simple to follow. There are *two* types of letter:

(a) *Business Letters* (b) *Personal Letters.*

BUSINESS LETTERS

Business letters are the sort of letters which you might send to a firm or to school or to someone you don't know, but with whom you have some business.

Here are some examples.

A letter of application for a job
A letter of complaint
A letter to the housing
    department
A letter to your local councillor

A letter to your headteacher
A letter to a newspaper
A letter to your bank manager
A letter asking for tickets for a
    football match or a pop concert

Here is an example of how a business letter is set out.

Sender's address **and** *date* **of letter.**

42 Coronation Drive,

Address **of person or firm you are writing to.**

Middleham.

23rd February 1980

Kwik-print Ltd.,

53 Crown Street,

Midchester.

Dear Sirs, ← **Salutation or greeting**

    I am to be married next August and would like to have my wedding invitations printed. ← *Content* **or** *message*

    Would you please send me some samples and your latest price list. There will be about eighty guests at the wedding.

          Yours faithfully,

Joan Roberts

Sometimes you can use 'Yours truly'

The *sender's signature*

You will notice that there are *two paragraphs* in *this* business letter.

EXERCISE 1

Copy out the letter on page 101 in your exercise book, but put in your own name and address, and today's date, as if you were the sender, instead of the examples given in the letter.

EXERCISE 2

Now copy out the letter again, in your exercise book. Again, use your own name and address and today's date. But this time, instead of the name and address of the firm given in the example, use this one:

Clearway Printers Ltd., 364 Castle Street, Eglington.

> *Show these exercises to your teacher.*

EXERCISE 3

In this exercise, you will be given certain information. Write this out in your exercise book, in the form of a business letter, as you did in the exercises above.

Name and address of the *sender*. (In all later exercises we will shorten this to *sender*)	Use your own name and address.
Date	Use today's date.
Person or firm to whom the letter is addressed. (In all later exercises we will shorten this to *addressee*)	Bonnyrig Brass & Silver Band Suppliers 40 Drum Street, Toothill.
What is to be said in the letter. (In all later exercises we will call this the *content*)	I would be obliged if you would supply me with an up-and-down trombone for a tall man with short arms, a left-handed triangle and three piccolos for Big Harry who thoroughly enjoyed the last ones.

> *Show the completed letter to your teacher.*

EXERCISE 4

Make up a letter of your own to the firm named below. Set it out as in the example letter on page 101.

SENDER: Use your own name and address and today's date.

ADDRESSEE: Odds, Bodds and Dodds Ltd.,
Penny Lane,
Bobsworth.

CONTENT: Make this up for yourself.
It can be funny, if you like.

Show this exercise to your teacher.

All *business letters* are written out in this way, but there is one important *change* you should notice.

If you are writing to a *particular person* instead of to a *firm*, you set it out like this:

---

116 Magnolia Buildings,

York Lane,

Westhampton.

6 March 1980

Ms Georgina Frappley,

Donkey Toys Ltd.,

36 High Street,

Shelford.

You know the *name* of the addressee so you use it in the *greeting*.

Dear Ms Frappley,

You may recall that last Wednesday when my wife and I visited your shop, you helped us choose a birthday present for our daughter. I would just like to tell you that she was thrilled with it. I will certainly recommend your shop to all our friends.

Because you know the actual name of the addressee you use 'Yours sincerely' instead of 'Yours faithfully'.

Yours sincerely,

Pat Muldoon

EXERCISE 5

Write out each of the following examples, in your exercise book, in the form of a business letter.
(There are two paragraphs in each letter.)

A. *Sender*

Use your own name and address.

Date

Use today's date.

Addressee

Mr Ironsides,
Cable Rope Works,
West Port, Cambuskennan.

Content

Would you please send me, at your earliest convenience, your latest wire-rope catalogue. I am thinking of crossing Niagara Falls the hard way.

B. *Sender*

Mr Daniel K Weasy,
116 Norton Avenue,
Nettleton.

Date

Use today's date.

Addressee

Ms Margaret Wishbone,
Queensway Restaurant,
82 Hickleton Street,
East Mumpley.

Content

Last Friday my wife and I had a meal in your restaurant. I am sure you would like to know that the doctor has now said that we are both out of danger.

Check your answers on page 148.

JOB APPLICATIONS

Another important type of *business letter* is the letter of application for a job. At some time in your life, you will have to write a letter applying for one. It might be as you prepare to leave school, or even for a temporary job in the school holidays.

Although employers will usually want to see you in person for an interview before they finally decide whether to employ you or not, they will usually ask you to *apply in writing*. This means writing a *business letter* to them.

Politeness, neatness and punctuality are essential if you want to make a good impression at an interview for a job. In writing a *letter of application* for a job, these three qualities are also necessary.

You should be polite in your letter.   *Politeness.*
You should set-out your letter *neatly.*   *Neatness.*
You should write *promptly.*   *Punctuality.*

An advertisement in a newspaper or on a notice-board, will usually tell you to *whom* you should address your letter (the *addressee*) in a firm or business.

Many large firms and businesses generally have a *Personnel Manager* or *Officer*, whose job it is to deal with applications and appointments. Sometimes you are asked to write *directly* to a *named person*.

Here is a typical example of an advertisement in a newspaper.

TEMPORARY STAFF REQUIRED

for busy Garden Centre work,
available from now until late Sept.
Would suit young students or school-
leavers. Apply in writing to:

**Green Fingers Garden Centre,
Primula Way,
Plantford.**

Evening Gazette 23/3/80

EXERCISE 6

Write out this letter of application, *in your exercise book, using your own* name and address *and the date* 23rd March 1980.

Green Fingers Garden Centre
Primula Way
Plantford

Always state the particular job you are applying for.

Dear Sir,

Temporary Staff: Green Fingers Garden Centre

I wish to apply for a job as one of your temporary staff, as advertised in the 'Evening Gazette' of 23rd March 1980.

I am seventeen years of age and recently left Plantford County High School. In October I hope to go to Middleham Technical College to start training as a landscape gardener and would appreciate the opportunity to gain some experience working with plants and gardening equipment.

Mr Perkins, my former Housemaster at school, has kindly agreed to give me a reference if it is required.

Yours faithfully,

Notice that in this letter, the *applicant* gives some details about his/her interests and circumstances. It is always a good idea to give information of this type to a possible employer. Notice also that the letter is set out neatly in *paragraphs.*

EXERCISE 7

Here are three more examples of advertisements which might interest you if you were searching for a job. You can find many examples for yourself in your local newspaper.

Using your own name and address and today's date, write out the letters of application for these three advertised jobs, in your exercise book. Remember to set them out correctly and neatly as you have been shown.

Laboratory Technicians:

Large international chemical firm, opening a new advanced factory in Midchester, require trainee laboratory technicians in their Polyester Division. Scientific qualifications and interest essential. Write for details to:

Personnel Officer,
POLY-CHEMIX LTD. (UK),
Balmoral Industrial Estate,
Midchester MR3 4PG.

Dear Sir,

TEAM MANAGER:

Struggling First Division League Club invite applications for the post of Team Manager. Full control of coaching and team selection. Write giving full details of age, experience and present salary.

Apply: *The Secretary,*
Midchester Albion F.C.,
Highfield Park,
Midchester MR5 1BQ

Dear Sir,

HAIRDRESSER

Modern city-centre salon requires junior hairdressing trainee. Full training given. Would suit recent school-leaver. Good wages and conditions offered. Apply in writing:

SUZI'S SALON
292 High Street,
Permham PM2 11R

Dear Madam,

Show your completed letters to your teacher.

SUPPLEMENTARY EXERCISES

Look up a copy of your local newspaper. Find the section which deals with job vacancies. *Select* two different *jobs advertised and write* letters *of* application *to the firms or businesses concerned, in your exercise book.*

> Show your completed letters to your teacher.

Here are some useful words to use when writing letters applying for a job. Care is required with spelling in these letters.

interview	available	details
qualifications	grateful	trainee
experience	faithfully	industrial
certificate	apprenticeship	recommendation
salary	reference	convenience
domestic	application	

Unit 3

PERSONAL LETTERS

Personal letters are the sort of letters you send to your friends or to members of your family, or to neighbours.

Here are some examples.

A letter to your Mum from a holiday abroad.

A letter to your sister in Canada.

A letter to your friend who is in hospital.

A letter to your uncle thanking him for the present which he sent you for Christmas.

A *personal letter* is set out like this.

Sender's address and date. ———➤ 24 Blossom Street,
Rosethorpe.
12th May 1980

The addressee's address is *not* needed in a personal letter.

Dear Agnes,   Christian name of addressee.

    I was delighted to receive your letter and look forward very much to seeing you. The weather here has been glorious for the last few days, so don't bother bringing a brolly with you!

    I will meet you at Rosethorpe Station on 22nd May at 11.15 am, as you suggest in your letter.

        Yours sincerely,

        Madeleine

EXERCISE 1

Write out, in your exercise book, each of the following examples in the form of a personal letter.

A. *Sender*

Date
Addressee

John McPherson,
8 Westcliff Circle,
Kirkhaven.
Use today's date.
Ms Noreen MacIntyre,
4 Gregor Drive,
Glencurran.

(Ms MacIntyre is John's aunt.)

Content

Thank you very much for the lovely model-kit which you sent me in hospital. I hope to have the plaster removed from my arm soon. I will enjoy making up the model fishing boat very much when I am allowed home

B. *Sender*
Date
Addressee

Use your *own* name and address.
Use today's date.
The letter is to your sister who is in hospital.

Content

I hope that you are feeling well after your operation.
Dad and I will come and see you after the match on Saturday.
I will bring some of those soft-centres which you like so much.

> *Show these letters to your teacher.*

Now you know *how* to set out a letter, but, of course, your letters will not always be as *short* as the ones we have used as examples.

We will now look at how to organise your letters into *sections*, or *paragraphs*.

Here is a simple business letter, with only *two* paragraphs.

---

16 Belmont Place,

Springdale.

14 October 1980

Electroflex Ltd.,

Mainspring Road,

Midcastle.

Dear Sirs,

(1)   Please send me one of your new Magi-Brushes which I saw advertised on television the other night.

(2)   I enclose my Postal Order for £1.75 and look forward to receiving my Magi-Brush.

Yours faithfully,

John Graham

Paragraph 1 This paragraph tells *what it is you want.*
Paragraph 2 This paragraph tells *what you have done.*

EXERCISE 1

In the following examples, the content *is written as though it were* one *paragraph, when, in fact, there should be two paragraphs. In your exercise book, write out the examples which follow, in the form of a letter. Remember each letter has* two *paragraphs. Remember also* what happens *when you write to a person whose* actual name is known to you. Use *today's date each time.*

A. *Sender*   Use your *own* name and address.

    Addressee   Bondiflo Gas and Bottle Co.,
South Windings Estate,
Shedford.

    Content

I would be obliged if you would send me a dozen bottles of Glo-Low, The Magic Cleanser, which my dog Toby and I enjoy very much. I enclose my cheque for £7.50 which includes postage and packing.

B. *Sender*   Mr Arthur Blunderstone,
62 Old Crow Road,
Bumbleton.

    Addressee   Ms Jemima Snufflebit,
Saddletree Riding School,
Quickpenny Walk,
Bumbleton.

    Content

My daughter, Imogen, is very keen on horses and would like to become a member of your Riding School. I hope that you will consider her application. Mr Trodgrass, who was her last teacher, says that Imogen is a promising pupil. He said that she could go a long way and he hoped she would.

C. *Sender*

Ms Angela Softheart,
90 Pitt Crescent,
Eglington.

Addressee

Mr Herbert Martin,
Douglas Park Comprehensive School,
Walker Avenue,
Eglington.

Content

Please excuse Billy for being absent from school yesterday. He had a slight cold. The doctor says that he should be able to return to school on Monday.

D. *Sender*

Mr Herbert Martin
(as above)

Addressee

Ms Angela Softheart
(as above)

Content

I am sorry to hear that Billy has a slight cold. No doubt he caught it when he took off his jacket on Monday to have a fight with Mickey Mallon. The Headteacher and I would be pleased if you would call along with Billy on Monday morning as we have a few things to discuss with you both, not least the injuries inflicted on Master Mallon.

Now check with the correct answers on pages 149–150.

LONGER LETTERS

Personal letters are the most pleasant of all to write. We do not have to be so stiff, or *formal* in our writing style. We can cover many more topics because friends or relations have more to say to each other than strangers would have to say. You will notice that there are, therefore, more paragraphs in this letter than in previous examples.

In this example of a longer letter (opposite) a young couple are writing to a former neighbour – from the United States of America to Britain.

> *Try these two exercises and then show them to your teacher.*

EXERCISE 2

In your exercise book, write out a plan of this letter showing the main point of each paragraph.
(There are five paragraphs in this letter.)

EXERCISE 3

Write Andy's reply to his old friends telling them what is happening at this time of year in Britain. Write the letter in your exercise book, making up an address of your own. Remember to write in paragraphs.

> *Show these completed exercises to your teacher.*

You should now be able to tackle letter-writing with confidence. Why not write a long *personal letter* to a friend, or relation, whom you have not seen for some time?

1645 East Fortune Drive,
Cresta Bay,
Miami, Florida,
U.S.A.
January 18th 1980.

Dear Andy,
A quick note, just to remind you that not everywhere is snow-bound at this time of the year. In fact, it's very summery weather here and we've been sunbathing and swimming this month. During the autumn, it was too hot to take full advantage of our time here but now the climate is very pleasant.

We have been to two American football games here - a very tough cross between rugby and gladiator fighting. You would be amazed by it!

We are hoping to tour the Space Centre at Cape Canaveral which is about three hundred kilometres from here, when Janet's brother, David, arrives in two weeks time.

Our trip to San Francisco and Los Angeles early last month was very interesting and exhausting. We came back via Phoenix and the Grand Canyon. It had always been an ambition of mine to visit it and now I can say I have done it!

If you are ever able to come and visit us here you can be sure of an extremely warm welcome and a free, guided tour of Florida.

With best wishes,
Love from
Terry, Janet and little Tracy.

Here is an example of a more formal longer letter. It is a letter to a newspaper from a reader. Perhaps one day you will write a letter to a newspaper and be lucky enough to have it published.

TIME TO SPARE

Dear Sir,

For ages we wanted to be able to live without television but, with four children, TV had become our main source of relaxation; and we felt we were stuck with it until the late 1980s at least.	*Paragraph 1* Television seemed necessary.
Then, on moving into a new house, our TV set was stolen. How we've longed to thank the thieves for doing us this inestimable service!	*Paragraph 2* Television set removed.
We're a different family now. We've made more friends and written more letters. Apart from these small changes our nine-year old son now takes violin lessons; the six-year old has become a bookworm; and my husband has found a new talent as a gardener.	*Paragraph 3* Changes which this brought to the family
As for myself, I'm to start learning Spanish at night school — something which, months ago, had been only a housewife's fancy.	*Paragraph 4* Changes which this brought to the writer.

Mrs H. G. Glasgow

EXERCISE 4

Using a plan, modelled on the one above, write a letter to the editor of a newspaper (the editor = Dear Sir,) about the unusual effects on you and your family of moving to a cottage which had no electricity supply.

> *Show this completed, planned letter to your teacher.*

MODULE 9

Direct Speech

Unit 1

INTRODUCTION

During a single day we all speak a great deal. We speak about sport, about pets, about school and about our families.

There are times when you want to put these *actual words* into *writing*. There is a special way of doing this in writing. It is called *Direct Speech*. Let us now look at how this is done.

It is very easy to do this in a strip cartoon. You simply put the *actual words* which a person is saying into what is called a *speech balloon*. The *speech balloon* points at the mouth of the speaker.

Example

However, in writing, we cannot put words inside balloons. This would take up a lot of space and would look silly. In writing, we put words inside *Speech Marks* like this " ".

The *Speech Marks* are on each side of the *actual words spoken*.

Spoken Words

Writing "Here is the News."

EXERCISE 1

Copy out in your exercise book, the actual words in the following examples, using speech marks instead of speech balloons.

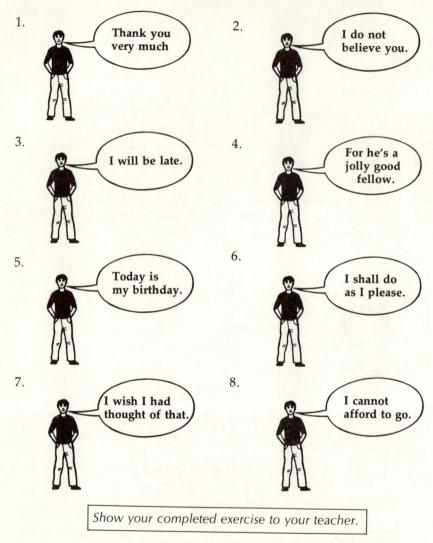

1.
Thank you very much

2.
I do not believe you.

3.
I will be late.

4.
For he's a jolly good fellow.

5.
Today is my birthday.

6.
I shall do as I please.

7.
I wish I had thought of that.

8.
I cannot afford to go.

Show your completed exercise to your teacher.

In these examples, it is easy to know *who* is *speaking*. We can see the balloon pointing to someone's mouth. In *writing*, however, we need to write down not only *what* was said (or the *actual words*) but also, *who* said it, and often *how* they said it.

Direct speech can be divided into two parts.

1. The part which tells you about the speaker – *who* he or she is and *how* they spoke.

We will call this the *personal part*.

This part is *not* put between speech marks.

2. The part which tells you *what* was said by the speaker.

We will call this the *Actual Words*.

This part *is* put between speech marks.

There are three main types of direct speech.

1. In the first type, the *Personal Part* goes *before* the *Actual Words*.

   This will be dealt with in *Unit 1*.

Personal Part	Actual Words

2. In the second type, the *Personal Part* goes *after* the *Actual Words*.

   This will be dealt with in *Unit 2*.

Actual Words	Personal Part

3. In the third type, the *Personal Part* goes in the *middle* of the *Actual Words*.

   This will be dealt with in *Unit 3*.

Actual Words	Personal Part	Actual Words

Speaker: Speech

Personal Part	Actual Words

Unit Test

Write out the following sentences in your exercise book, putting in the capitals and all punctuation marks, including speech marks.

1. the policeman asked may i see your driving licence
2. the referee replied any more of that and off you go
3. the mechanic said to me you need a new tyre
4. the doctor said i am going to give you a prescription
5. the old man shouted i will tell your parents
6. the conductor announced there are two seats upstairs

> *Check with the answers on page 151.*
> *If you made no mistakes, go to Unit 2 on page 125.*
> *If you made any mistakes, continue with this unit.*

In all sentences where the *Personal Part* comes *first* you put a *comma* (,) just *before* the *Actual Words*.

Example
    The little girl asked, "Can I go home now?"

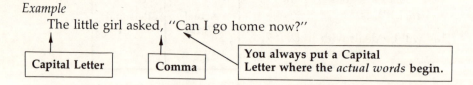

| **Capital Letter** | **Comma** | **You always put a Capital Letter where the *actual words* begin.** |

EXERCISE 1

Write out the following sentences in your exercise book, putting in all capitals, speech marks and commas.

1. the little boy muttered to himself one day my turn will come.
2. a doctor came on the scene and said i will see to this
3. the headteacher shook hands with me and said you have done extremely well
4. with tears streaming down his face cyril screamed i shall do as i please
5. the supporters chanted nice one cyril
6. jones gulped nervously as the customs officer stepped forward and said just one minute

120

7. while we watched the huge screen filled with flames and smoke and a voice said we have lift off
8. the two guards advanced along the corridor and one of them shouted we know you are in here somewhere
9. my opponent shook hands with me and said here's to the next time
10. an elderly man in a grey suit rushed into our office shouting i've been robbed
11. as if in a dream phyllis heard a voice say i now pronounce you man and wife
12. a bedraggled figure waited patiently for me to wind down the window of the car and said i am trying to reach inverness
13. throughout the evening we manned the pumps but just before midnight the chief engineer said its hopeless
14. it came as no surprise when the policeman said i am afraid that i have some very bad news
15. the martian climbed slowly down a little ladder and said in a high pitched whine take me to your leader

Check with the answers on page 151.

When the *Actual Words* end with a *question mark*, the rules are the same. You put a *comma* before the *Actual Words* and keep in the *question mark*.

Example

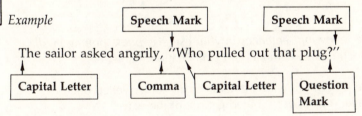

EXERCISE 2

Write out the following sentences in your exercise book, putting in all capitals, speech marks, commas *and* question marks.

1. the little man asked his wife timidly can i go out now
2. the army captain asked sweetly who is going to volunteer
3. the teacher asked the class wearily now do you understand
4. the stern-faced policeman asked can i see your licence
5. the young man asked the young girl do you come here often
6. the tourists asked anxiously is the castle haunted

7 the boy scout asked do you want to cross the road
8. the newsagent asked me do you want the papers cancelled
9. the manager asked me politely do you wish to complain
10. the interviewer asked me do you believe in the Loch Ness Monster

Check with the answers on page 152.

When the *Actual Words* end with an *exclamation mark*, the rules are the same.
You put a *comma* before the *Actual Words* and keep in the *exclamation mark*.

Example

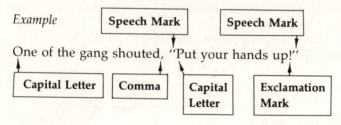

EXERCISE 3

Write out the following sentences in your exercise book, putting in all capitals, speech marks, commas *and* exclamation marks.

1. when he hit himself with the hammer my father yelled ouch
2. the enraged bus driver shouted get out of the way
3. the mad professor whispered this will make you big and strong
4. the football supporters chanted off
5. it came as quite a shock when cynthia cried get lost
6. the bell rang and the referee shouted seconds out
7. my friend charlie frowned as i exclaimed checkmate
8. all he could think of saying as the medal was placed around his neck was ta
9. the ice opened up beneath them and i heard them cry help
10. the audience applauded and cried hear hear

Check with the answers on page 152.

122

You have been writing out three different types of sentences in *Direct Speech*.

> 1. *Statements* – ending with a *period*
> 2. *Questions* – ending with a *question mark*
> 3. *Exclamations* – ending with an *exclamation mark*

Statement

The traffic warden stuck a ticket on the windscreen and said, "I am only doing my job."

Question

The traffic warden stuck a ticket on the windscreen and said, "Do you know you are my first customer today?"

Exclamation

The traffic warden stuck a ticket on the windscreen and said, "I don't care if you are the King of Siam!"

EXERCISE 4

Write out three sentences of your own. The first part of each sentence has been started for you. In each group you should have one statement, one question and one exclamation. Write them out in your exercise book.

A 1. Our next door neighbour leaned out of her window and said —
    2. Our next door neighbour leaned out of her window and asked —
    3. Our next door neighbour leaned out of her window and shouted —

B 1. The little man looked up at him and said —
    2. The little man looked up at him and asked —
    3. The little man looked up at him and shouted —

C 1. Jumping up and down the tousle-haired boy said —
    2. Jumping up and down the tousle-haired boy asked —
    3. Jumping up and down the tousle-haired boy shouted —

D 1. As the water started to come up over his shoes the captain said —
    2. As the water started to come up over his shoes the captain asked —
    3. As the water started to come up over his shoes the captain shouted —

E 1. The photographer popped his head from behind his camera and said
—

2. The photographer popped his head from behind his camera and asked
—

3. The photographer popped his head from behind his camera and shouted —

Show this exercise to your teacher.

EXERCISE 5

Now that you have grasped the idea, put in the full punctuation marks in the following sentences. Write them out in your exercise book.
Notice that some of them contain statements, *some contain* questions *and some contain* exclamations

1. the doctor studied the X-ray plates carefully and said i've got some good news for you
2. i felt very flattered when some kids came up and asked can we have your autograph
3. the chairman picked me out of the audience and asked what is your question
4. the whole town cheered as the lone ranger rode off into the sunset crying hi-ho silver
5. the receptionist ran her finger down the page and asked sweetly what is your name again
6. whenever things are going really badly i say to myself worse things happen at sea

Check with the answers on page 152.

Unit 2 Speech: Speaker

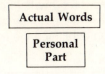

Unit Test

Write out the following sentences in your exercise book, putting in the capitals and all punctuation marks, including speech marks.

1. i think you have dialled the wrong number replied the operator
2. hooray yelled the excited youngsters
3. where is your absence note asked the teacher
4. tell me all about it said my granny
5. how many times do i have to tell you mumbled the prisoner
6. what a load of rubbish echoed round the stadium

> *Check with the answers on page 153.*
> *If you made no mistakes, go to Unit 3 on page 128.*
> *If you made any mistakes, continue with this unit.*

Sometimes we need to put the *Actual Words* first and the *Personal Part* second. We often do this to make our writing more interesting. When the *Actual Words* end with a *period* we change this *final period* into a *comma*. Notice that you do *not* use a *capital letter* at the start of the *Personal Part*.

Example

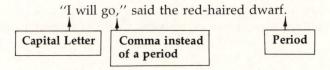

EXERCISE 1

Write out the following sentences in your exercise book, putting in all capitals, speech marks, commas and periods.

1. at last i will have a home of my own he thought
2. i have been off work for the last two weeks said my friend
3. you will have to make another appointment explained the nurse
4. i have nothing to say at this point muttered the prime minister

5. whatever you do don't panic i said to myself
6. grass doesn't grow on a busy street answered my bald cousin
7. i think i've lost my pension book sobbed the old lady
8. you will have to produce your passport explained the travel agent

Check with the answers on page 153.

 When the *Actual Words* end with a *question mark*, the rules are the same. Notice that you do *not* use a *capital letter* at the start of the *Personal Part*.

Example   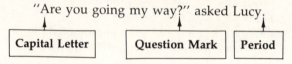 "Are you going my way?" asked Lucy.

| Capital Letter | Question Mark | Period |

EXERCISE 2

Write out the following sentences in your exercise book, putting in all capitals, speech marks, commas and question marks.

1. what on earth do you mean asked mr jones
2. can i go out and play asked tommy
3. could i have my bill now said the american tourist
4. where did you go after the match asked my mother
5. can i leave the table now asked his daughter
6. where does it hurt inquired the doctor
7. when would you like to leave the island continued our host
8. could you open your mouth a little wider please whispered my dentist

Check with the answers on page 153.

 When the *Actual Words* end with an *exclamation mark*, the rules are the same. Notice that you do *not* use a *capital letter* at the start of the *Personal Part*.

Example   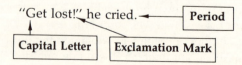 "Get lost!" he cried. ◄——— Period

| Capital Letter | Exclamation Mark |

EXERCISE 3

Write out the following sentences in your exercise book, putting in all capitals, speech marks, commas *and* exclamation marks.

1. look out yelled his father
2. hands up snarled the bandit
3. read all about it shouted the news-boy
4. stand and deliver cried dick turpin
5. i submit moaned his opponent
6. cut out the rough stuff ordered the referee
7. but i didn't take his wallet insisted billy
8. turn that radio off yelled my neighbour

Check with the answers on page 153.

When there are *two, or more,* sentences in the *Actual Words*, only the *final period* is changed into a *comma*.

Example

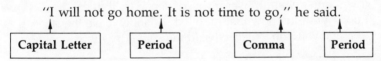

| Capital Letter | Period | Comma | Period |

EXERCISE 4

Write out the following sentences in your exercise book, putting in full punctuation marks.
(Notice that there are two *sentences in the* actual words.)

1. you have been found guilty of a very serious crime i sentence you to five years imprisonment said the judge
2. i am really very sorry i don't know what came over me said the prisoner
3. i am becoming quite deaf speak up a bit roared my uncle
4. your father was a good man we shall not see his like again said mr brown sadly

5. that's all i can tell you at the moment i hope to give you further information in the morning said the captain
6. you can stop worrying now we've landed safely said the pilot's calm voice.

Check with the answers on page 154.

Unit 3 Speech: Speaker: Speech

Unit Test

Write out the following sentences in your exercise book, putting in capitals and all punctuation marks, including speech marks.

1. i will not go he said for you or for anyone
2. i don't really care he replied one way or the other
3. but tell me she asked what is the real reason
4. if you don't wrap up warmly said alena you'll freeze
5. i don't wish to know that i replied so kindly leave the stage
6. if at first you don't succeed said the spider try try try again

Check with the answers on page 154.
If you made no mistakes report to your teacher.
If you made any mistakes, continue with this unit.

When the *Actual Words* contain only *one sentence,* with the *Personal Part* in the middle, this is how you do it:

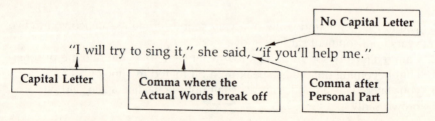

128

You do this whether the *Actual Words* contain a *statement*, a *question* or an *exclamation*. Here are *two* further examples, using the *question mark* and the *exclamation mark*:–

? "After you go," she sobbed, "what will become of me?"

! "I will die," he cried, "but not surrender!"

EXERCISE 1

Write out the following sentences in your exercise book, putting in capitals and full punctuation marks.

1. if you are going to the shops she asked will you buy me some fruit gums
2. despite my appalling rudeness he pleaded can you find it in your heart to forgive me
3. stay in bed for a couple of days ordered my doctor unless you want to catch pneumonia
4. hard to port yelled the skipper or we'll hit the iceberg
5. if you want to reach bristol tonight explained the porter you'll have to change at crewe
6. if you promise not to tell a soul whispered agatha i'll let you into a little secret

> *Check with the answers on page 154.*

Sometimes, there are *two, or more*, sentences in the *Actual Words* and *one* of them finishes at the *Personal Part*.

Example

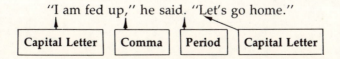

"I am fed up," he said. "Let's go home."

| Capital Letter | Comma | Period | Capital Letter |

EXERCISE 2

Write out the following sentences in your exercise book, putting in the capitals *and* full punctuation marks.

1. thank you for all your help said my neighbour i'll try to repay it some day
2. do exactly as i say whispered the sinister stranger you'll just have to trust me
3. i don't believe it repeated the taxidermist i simply don't believe it
4. could you give me a lift to london said the red-faced man i will pay you well
5. don't just stand there yelled my father come into the house at once

Check with the answers on page 155.

ANSWERS

The Apostrophe

Unit 1

Unit Test (page 10)

1. My mother's sisters are coming today.
2. The horse's neck was glistening with sweat.
3. He kicked his opponent's ankle.
4. The teacher's books were lying on the girl's desk.
5. What is the doctor's number?
6. The children's cries were not heard.

EXERCISE 1 (page 11)

1. The hand is pointing at the dog's tail.
2. The hand is pointing at the dog's eye.
3. The hand is pointing at the dog's back.
4. The hand is pointing at the dog's nose.
5. The hand is pointing at the dog's collar.
6. The hand is pointing at the dog's leg.

EXERCISE 3 (page 12)

1. The tree's leaves
2. The kettle's spout
3. The train's whistle
4. The boy's trousers
5. The ship's bottom
6. The butcher's boy
7. The doctor's visit
8. The chorus-girl's smile
9. The sun's glow
10. The boxer's gloves
11. The jury's verdict
12. The American's passport
13. The typewriter's ribbon
14. The rifle's trigger
15. The postman's knock

Unit 2

Unit Test (page 13)

1. The monkeys' paws were wet.
2. The cars' axles were covered in dust.
3. The cricketers' coats lay on the ground.
4. The soldiers' rifles lay in a heap.
5. The twins' faces were exactly alike.
6. The children's presents were under the Christmas tree.

(NOTE The plural form *children* does not end in *s*, so it becomes *children's*.)

EXERCISE 1 (page 13)

1. The hands are pointing at the cats' bowls.
2. The hands are pointing at the cats' ears.
3. The hands are pointing at the cats' legs.
4. The hands are pointing at the cats' eyes.
5. The hands are pointing at the cats' collars.
6. The hands are pointing at the cats' tails.

EXERCISE 2 (page 14)

1. The horses' backs
2. The schoolboys' blazers
3. The grocers' shops
4. The old ladies' hats
5. The supporters' bus
6. For goodness' sake
7. The pipers' bonnets
8. The fiddlers' elbows
9. The churches' bells
10. The bottles' corks
11. The cities' Chief Constables

Unit 3

Unit Test (page 15)

1. I'm not sure where I put it.
2. There's a gale warning on the radio.
3. We're late for school!
4. Shouldn't you take out the plug first?
5. Can't you see what I'm doing?
6. He's one of the best goalkeepers in the country.

EXERCISE 1 (page 16)

Full Expression	Shortened Form
1. there is	there's
2. I am	I'm
3. is not	isn't
4. were not	weren't
5. that is	that's
6. should not	shouldn't
7. you will	you'll
8. have not	haven't
9. where is	where's
10. what is	what's
11. we are	we're
12. they are	they're
13. I shall/will	I'll
14. are not	aren't
15. we shall/will	we'll
16. would not	wouldn't
17. had not	hadn't
18. you would	you'd
19. I had	I'd
20. who is	who's

EXERCISE 2 (page 17)

1. Who's your friend?
2. He's no friend of mine; that's my brother.
3. Who's been eating my porridge?
4. It's that girl from next door again!
5. I'd walk a million miles for one of your smiles.
6. You'll never walk alone.
7. Who'd have believed it?
8. Here's your hat. What's your hurry?
9. I wouldn't like to be in your shoes.
10. They're all I've got.

The Sentence

Unit 1

EXERCISE 5 (page 21)

1. The teacher told us to open our books.
2. Freezing fog caused the pile-up on the motorway.
3. The doctor told me to stay in bed for a few days.
4. Suddenly Tom had a brilliant idea.
5. The passengers were asked to board the aircraft.

Unit 2

EXERCISE 1 (page 21)

1. The lion roared. The hyena took off.
2. The winger crossed the ball. The centre scored.
3. I'm Tarzan. She is Jane.
4. I saw a giraffe. It was as big as a house.
5. The fire engine raced to the fire. The siren was howling.
6. Seven threes are twenty-one. Seven fours are twenty-eight.
7. My bicycle was stolen this morning. The police have a full description of it.
8. There will be rain in northern areas of the country tonight. Tomorrow will be bright and sunny everywhere.

EXERCISE 2 (page 22)

1. The spaceship turned round. The laser beam slid past into space. The crew breathed a sigh of relief.
2. The best football teams have a good manager. The manager's job is to buy the players and pick the team. It is the trainer's job to make sure the team is fit.
3. The hunter stood stock still. The rhinoceros looked this way and that with his little pig eyes. Then he charged.
4. I once saw the great Evel Knievel. He leapt over fourteen cars on his motor-bike. When he landed, his bike broke into a million bits and he was lucky to be thrown clear.

5. Lemmings are tiny creatures a bit like mice. They say that every so often large numbers of them commit suicide for no reason by throwing themselves over a cliff. I think it's a lot of rubbish myself.

EXERCISE 3 (page 22)

1. At break Billy went out into the yard. The wind cutting straight across from the playing fields made him turn his back and raise a shoulder while he looked around for a sheltered place. All the corners were occupied.

2. I went out of doors and looked round. The air was pure. A cliff on the edge of the aerodrome stood in profile against the sky as if it were daylight. Over the desert reigned a vast silence as of a house in order.

3. I got up and wandered as sadly as I could to the door of the church. I went inside. There were some people kneeling in some of the pews. I tiptoed down the aisle to nearly the front row and sat in one of the pews myself. I didn't kneel but sat with my head bowed. I closed my eyes and thought of the vicar coming up and putting his hand on my shoulder and asking me if he could do anything.

4. There were seven puppies in the team. The others had been born earlier in the year and were nine and ten months old while White Fang was only eight months old. Each dog was fastened to the sled by a single rope. No two ropes were of the same length while the difference in length between any two ropes was at least that of a dog's body. Every rope was brought to a ring at the front end of the sled.

5. After some hours the troop reached a lonely hacienda. A hacienda is a large farm and being enclosed by a stout high wall it stands up like a small fortress in the country round. They rode into the spacious farm yard and dismounted in order to rest themselves a bit. The owner of the hacienda came out and the officer asked whether he had seen anything of a party of mounted men. The man declared that no one could have ridden past the place without his knowing it. Whereupon the officer informed him that he would have to search the hacienda and the owner replied that he might do as he liked and went back into the house. The troopers were about to follow him when they were met by a volley from different parts of the house. By the time they had retreated through the yard gates they had four wounded and one dead.

Unit 3

Unit Test-Comma Splice (page 24)

1. George looked at his watch. It was twenty past nine.
2. An upstairs door banged shut. Outside the wind howled.
3. Sheila decided not to buy the oranges in the supermarket. They were cheaper in the corner shop.
4. My mother accused me of lying to her. I did not know what she would do next.
5. The driver pressed his foot hard on the brake-pedal. His taxi was completely out of control.
6. The nurse told me not to worry about the operation. Her smile cheered me up for the rest of the day.

EXERCISE 2 (page 26)

1. We jumped out of the aircraft at midnight. My parachute opened easily and I could see the others drifting towards the ground. There was a full moon and I could make out white markers quite clearly below me in the field. There were a number of people running out of a small wood to greet us. They were waving their arms in the air.

2. Many people find it difficult to write in proper sentences. They often forget to put a capital letter at the beginning of a sentence and a period at the end of a sentence. This means their writing is confused and it does not always make sense.

3. With a telephone you can chat to friends and make last minute arrangements. You can keep in touch with your family, make bookings, ring the shops and call the plumber or electrician at the first sign of trouble. Then, of course, other people can ring you. Most of their calls will be friendly chats but sometimes a message can be vital. It's then that a phone can save you hours of frustration, a wasted journey or missed appointment.

Unit Test-Capital Letters (page 26)

1. I hope to go on holiday to Spain next year.
2. My dog Goldie had pups last November.
3. Glasgow is situated on the River Clyde.
4. Our teacher read to us from Treasure Island by Robert Louis Stevenson.
5. Last Sunday we visited our cousins in Newcastle.
6. The Rosewell Youth Club meets every Monday and Friday, except in the holiday months of July and August.

EXERCISE 1 (page 27)

1. In 1980, the Olympic Games were held in Moscow.
2. When I was on holiday in New York last September, I was able to visit the United Nations building.
3. Sally and James Flannigan organised a dance in aid of Oxfam.
4. We have a copy of the Oxford English Dictionary in our school library.
5. Hank Fielding's song, Golden Corn, appeared in the Top Twenty three weeks running.
6. Next Tuesday I have an appointment with Mr Foster who is the area manager for Smith and Jones.
7. Watership Down is an unusual story about rabbits which has been translated into many languages.
8. Thirty days hath September, April, June and November.
9. Aunt Margaret introduced me to her neighbours, the Thomsons, when I visited her last Thursday.
10. The Queen narrowly missed injury when her official car skidded into a lamp-post on Waterloo Bridge this morning.

Spelling One

Unit 3

EXERCISE 16 (page 41)

1. The car was *stationary* at the kerb-side.
2. A good secretary always has a full supply of *stationery*.
3. We bought special *stationery* for my sister's wedding last summer.
4. Someone ran into us while we were *stationary* at the lights.
5. *Stationery* includes paper and envelopes.

Spelling Two

Unit 1

EXERCISE 1 (page 42)

1. saddest
2. beginning
3. referring
4. equalled
5. preferring
6. modelled
7. jewellery
8. regrettable
9. occurrence
10. pencilled
11. beginner
12. modelling
13. regretted
14. occurring
15. preferred

EXERCISE 4 (page 44)

1. equalling
2. happened
3. modelled, modelling
4. preferred
5. regretting
6. occurred, occurring
7. benefited, benefiting
8. referred, referring

Unit 3

EXERCISE 9 (page 50)

1. lorries
2. cities
3. boundaries
4. communities
5. cherries
6. dictionaries
7. butterflies
8. libraries
9. duties
10. industries
11. memories
12. qualities
13. quantities
14. centuries
15. families

EXERCISE 10 (page 50)

1. lorry, lorries
2. family, families
3. quality, qualities
4. memory, memories
5. century, centuries
6. dictionary, dictionaries
7. cherry, cherries
8. industry, industries

EXERCISE 12 (page 51)

1. beautiful
2. noisily
3. merciless
4. carried
5. burial
6. marriage
7. defiance
8. happiness
9. craftily
10. mysterious

EXERCISE 13 (page 52)

1. marrying
2. carrying
3. studying
4. defying
5. flying

EXERCISE 14 (page 52)

1. merciless
2. carrying
3. tried
4. happiness
5. mysterious
6. flying
7. likelihood
8. studying

Spelling Three

Unit 1

EXERCISE 1 (page 53)

1. famous
2. movable
3. separated
4. pleasurable
5. writing

6. exciting
7. valuable
8. believed
9. received
10. fascinating

Unit 3

EXERCISE 13 (page 61)

1. exactly
2. specially
3. beautifully
4. sincerely
5. dangerously

6. immediately
7. separately
8. quickly
9. entirely
10. cruelly

The Comma

Unit 1

Unit Test (page 77)

1. Sammy put his trunks, towel, goggles and flippers into the locker.
2. The clinic will open on Mondays, Tuesdays, Thursdays and Saturday morning.
3. The stranger was a tall, lean, weather-beaten man.
4. My car needed a new exhaust, gearbox, radiator and two front tyres.
5. Spacious top-flat, containing living-room, kitchen, two bedrooms, bathroom.
6. We joined Mr Bromley, John and Mary Bennett, the Smith twins and Deirdre at the airport.

EXERCISE 2 (page 79)

1. The king's daughter was selfish, vain and very unhappy.
2. My favourite breakfast is bacon, eggs, toast and a large mug of steaming hot tea.
3. My mother asked me to go to the shops and buy a paper, a box of matches, two bars of chocolate and a battery for the transistor.
4. Ground floor flat comprising living-room, three bedrooms, kitchen and bathroom.
5. There was a shortage of carrots, Brussels sprouts, cabbages and potatoes because of the recent severe frost.
6. Susan came fourth in the high jump, second in the long jump, third in the javelin and beat all the boys in the shot putt.
7. When asked to empty his pockets by the teacher, the wee boy produced two packets of bubble-gum, a rusty pen-knife, four sticks of chalk and the remains of a smoked sausage.
8. On the seventh day of Christmas my true-love gave to me, seven swans a-swimming, six geese a-laying, five gold rings, four calling birds, three French hens, two turtle doves and a partridge in a pear tree.

Unit 2

Unit Test (page 80)

1. I asked Tommy, the boy next-door, if he had seen our cat.
2. What you should do, of course, is to phone for the police.
3. The nurse, who had just come on duty, gave me a drink of water.
4. Mr Wong, the restaurant owner, showed us to a table near the window.
5. The burst pipe, which had thawed overnight, ruined his bedroom ceiling.
6. The world heavy-weight champion, aged thirty eight, retained his title in New York.

EXERCISE 2 (page 82)

1. Hans, who looked after the animals, caught the thieves.
2. Toby, the clown's little dog, made the audience roar with laughter.
3. The audience, which was made up of children, laughed loudly.
4. Sally, the ice-cream girl, never missed a show.
5. The circus security man, whose name was Rolf, loved Maria, the trapeze artist.
6. One little boy, who was a trouble-maker, hit the lion with a marble.
7. Zorro, the Sword Swallower, who had recently arrived from Spain, cut himself shaving and could not appear that afternoon.
8. Mr Spangler, who was also one of the clowns, hurriedly changed into a pair of baggy trousers and a ragged shirt.

Unit 3

Unit Test (page 83)

1. My sister apologised to me, but I know she didn't mean it.
2. A comma is used to separate items in a list, as shown in Unit 1.
3. It will be generally dull and cloudy tomorrow, though temperatures will be above average for the time of year.
4. The trapper decided to press on to Red River Falls, which was twenty miles farther north.
5. When the exam finished, the teacher told us to put our pens away and leave the room quietly.
6. The rescue team set off up the mountain, although they knew there was little chance of finding any survivors.

143

EXERCISE 1 (page 84)

1. Before Mary washed her hair, she came downstairs.
2. Mary washed her hair, before she came downstairs.
3. Before Mary came downstairs, she washed her hair.
4. Mary came downstairs, before she washed her hair.

EXERCISE 2 (page 84)

1. The little girl laughed, when her pal slipped on a banana skin.
2. I have been trying to help you, although you do not realise it.
3. John did what he was told, but Peter did not pay any attention.
4. The game was cancelled, as the pitch was waterlogged.
5. You should not swim after a heavy meal, because you might develop stomach cramp.
6. Several passengers received minor injuries, although it was a miracle that no one was killed.
7. The circus performer used to dive ten metres into a wet sponge, until one day he broke his neck.
8. He broke his neck, because someone had wrung out the sponge!

Supplementary Exercises

EXERCISE A (page 86)

Children Do keep matches, lighters, cigarettes out of their reach. Do not ever leave them alone in the home. Do guard all fires, radiators and stoves, and ensure that all heaters and electrical fires are in good order. Do keep flammable liquids such as petrol, paraffin, white spirit and methylated spirits outdoors in proper containers, and take care not to use paints or adhesives near a naked flame. Do not store combustibles such as newspapers, rags and boxes, especially under the stairs, in the attic or in similar places.
Before going to Bed Do switch off and unplug the TV set and all other appliances not in use, settle down coal or coke fires, checking that the fire guard is in position, and check that no cigarette ends are still burning. Do not forget, after making these checks, to close all doors and windows.

EXERCISE B (page 87)

1. Something appeared, not to the sides or behind, but almost directly in front of him. It was bright and moving incredibly fast and then it was firing just above him. Taken completely by surprise, the Imperial fighter came apart, just as its pilot realised what had happened.

2. Smith's room was small and oddly shaped, owing to its situation under the roof. It was as though the builder, arriving nearly at the summit of his labour, had come upon this extra space by surprise and on the spur of the moment had popped a door and a window to it, so's not to embarrass the stairs with leading to nowhere. A bed, a chest and a chair were the sole furnishings – and a pot of strong sweet herbs. For though Miss Mansfield could burn the sheets after Smith had slept in them, she could not burn the room, so the herbs were the next best thing.

3. Start cooking with gas and you've never felt so in command of things. That quick, clean, obedient, blue flame changes from the slightest simmer to fierce heat at the turn of your fingers. And because it's so easy to control gas, it's easy to control your fuel bill, too! Speedy, economical gas.

The Paragraph

EXERCISE 2 (page 91)

Apple Fritters

100 g self-raising flour; 1 standard egg, separated; about 125 ml tepid water; 1 very large cooking apple; lard or corn oil for deep frying; 30 g caster sugar, optional.

Sift the flour into a mixing bowl; make a hollow in the centre of the flour and add the egg yolk. Gradually add tepid water until you have a thick mixture (it should be stiff enough to coat the back of a wooden spoon).

Peel and core apple carefully. Cut into 8 thin rings.

Gently heat the pan of lard or oil. Whisk egg white until very stiff and snowy then fold into the batter. Dip the apple slices into the batter and deep fry in hot oil, 4 at a time, for about 2 minutes, or until they are puffed up and golden.

Drain on absorbent kitchen paper. If you're using sugar, sprinkle it on the fritters and serve.

EXERCISE 6 (page 97)

A. Holbein Holiday Apartments

The Holbein Holiday Apartments are ideally situated in the principal hotel area of San Antonio, and that's an open invitation to explore the many dances and entertainments which make this resort one of the happiest holiday spots under the sun.

Each apartment contains 2 bedrooms separated by a splendidly styled bathroom. The living/dining area is a clever blend of rich dark woods and complementary coloured tiles, tastefully furnished, to suit 5 guests (an extra bed can be accommodated in the living area).

The 15 minute walk to town takes you past an interesting variety of hotels, traditional homes and bars while the beach is only 600 metres away.

Kitchen fittings and equipment are ultra-modern for ease and efficiency including cooker, grill, fridge, pots, pans, cutlery, china etc.

The balcony is spacious and if you can forego its natural sunny attractions, all the facilities of the popular and lively Hotel Putchet are directly over the road – and the swimming pool is a challenge in itself.

B. Salmon Fishing (page 98)

By this time, I had seen more than enough of salmon nets, but we were not finished with them yet. The dirty bag net Big Willie and I had been working on before dinner had to be lifted from the river bank, and spread on the grass of the drying green.

I realised then that the sea was the master of the salmon fishing. As fast as we cleaned and dried the nets, we had to start packing the day's catch in ice for the boat from Portree called for the fish every Wednesday and Saturday.

Back and forwards we plodded, between the store shed and the river, lugging the heavy fish boxes aboard the coble. We were taking the last two boxes down when Long John called that the boat was coming.

She was barely in sight, no more than a small speck in the south, but by the time we had put out in the coble, I was able to make out her covered wheelhouse. She was a converted fishing boat, well suited for the job of transporting the salmon to Portree.

EXERCISE 7 (a) (page 99)

Ali Baba was a poor woodcutter, who lived in a small town in Persia very many years ago and who earned his living by selling wood in the market place.

One day as he was riding his mule through the forest on his way home, he saw an enormous cloud of dust which seemed to be moving towards him. As it got nearer it turned out to be a troop of horsemen, so Ali Baba got off his mule and climbed up into a tree to hide, fearing they might be robbers.

Robbers they were indeed, forty of them, and they rode past the tree where Ali was hiding, alighted from their horses outside a huge rock, and removed their saddle-bags which seemed to be very heavy.

Then Ali Baba heard the man at the head of the troop (apparently the leader) call out in a loud voice the words, "Open Sesame!" and to his great astonishment, a huge door in the rock opened slowly and all forty robbers went inside carrying their loaded saddle-bags.

Unit 2

EXERCISE 5 (page 104)

A.

Mr Ironsides,   **Your own address**
Cable Rope Works,   **Today's date**
West Port,
Cambuskennan.

Dear Mr Ironsides,

        Would you please send me, at your earliest
convenience, your latest wire-rope catalogue.

        I am thinking of crossing Niagara Falls the hard
way.

        Yours sincerely,

        Your signature

B.

Ms Margaret Wishbone,   116 Norton Avenue
Queensway Restaurant,   Nettleton
82 Hickleton Street   **Today's date**
East Mumpley.

Dear Ms Wishbone,

        Last Friday my wife and I had a meal in
your restaurant.

        I am sure you would like to know that the doctor
has now said that we are both out of danger.

        Yours sincerely,

        Daniel K. Weary

Unit 3

EXERCISE 1 (pages 112–113)

A.

```
Bondiflo Gas and Bottle Co.,        Your own address
South Windings Estate,              Today's date
Shedford.

Dear Sir,
          I would be obliged if you would send me a dozen
bottles of Glo-Low - The Magic Cleanser which my dog, Toby,
and I enjoy very much.
          I enclose my cheque for £7.50 which includes postage
and packing.

          Yours faithfully,

          Your signature
```

B.

```
                                    62 Old Crow Road,
                                    Bumbleton.
Ms Jemima Snufflebit,               Today's date
Saddletree Riding School,
Quickpenny Walk,
Bumbleton.

Dear Ms Snufflebit,
          My daughter, Imogen, is very keen on horses and
would like to become a member of your Riding School.  I hope
that you will consider her application.
          Mr Trodgrass, who was her last teacher, says
that Imogen is a promising pupil.  He said that she could go a
long way and he hoped she would.

          Yours sincerely,

          Arthur Blunderstone
```

C.

90 Pitt Crescent,
Eglington.

Today's date

Mr Herbert Martin,

Douglas Park Comprehensive School,

Walker Avenue,

Eglington.

Dear Mr Martin,

      Please excuse Billy for being absent from school yesterday. He had a slight cold.

      The doctor says that he should be able to return to school on Monday.

      Yours sincerely,

Angela Softheart

D.

Douglas Park Comp.School
Walker Avenue,
Eglington.

Today's date

Ms Angela Softheart,

90 Pitt Crescent,

Eglington.

Dear Ms Softheart,

      I am sorry to hear that Billy has a slight cold. No doubt he caught it when he took off his jacket on Monday to have a fight with Mickey Mallon.

      The Headteacher and I would be pleased if you would call along with Billy on Monday morning as we have a few things to discuss with you both, not least the injuries inflicted on Master Mallon.

      Yours sincerely,

Herbert Martin

Direct Speech

Unit 1

Unit Test (page 120)

1. The policeman asked, "May I see your driving licence?"
2. The referee replied, "Any more of that and off you go."
3. The mechanic said to me, "You need a new tyre."
4. The doctor said, "I am going to give you a prescription."
5. The old man shouted, "I will tell your parents!"
6. The conductor announced, "There are two seats upstairs."

EXERCISE 1 (page 120)

1. The little boy muttered to himself, "One day my turn will come."
2. A doctor came on the scene and said, "I will see to this."
3. The headteacher shook hands with me and said, "You have done extremely well."
4. With tears streaming down his face Cyril screamed, "I shall do as I please."
5. The supporters chanted, "Nice one, Cyril."
6. Jones gulped nervously as the Custom's officer stepped forward and said, "Just one minute."
7. While we watched, the huge screen filled with flames and smoke and a voice said, "We have lift off."
8. The two guards advanced along the corridor and one of them shouted, "We know you are in here somewhere."
9. My opponent shook hands with me and said, "Here's to the next time."
10. An elderly man in a grey suit rushed into our office shouting, "I've been robbed."
11. As if in a dream Phyllis heard a voice say, "I now pronounce you man and wife."
12. A bedraggled figure waited patiently for me to wind down the window of the car and said, "I'm trying to get to Inverness."
13. Throughout the evening we manned the pumps but just before midnight the chief engineer said, "It's hopeless."
14. It came as no surprise when the policeman said, "I'm afraid that I have some very bad news for you."
15. The Martian climbed slowly down a little ladder and said in a high-pitched whine, "Take me to your leader."

EXERCISE 2 (page 121)

1. The little man asked his wife timidly, "Can I go out now?"
2. The army captain asked sweetly, "Who is going to volunteer?"
3. The teacher asked the class wearily, "Now do you understand?"
4. The stern-faced policeman asked, "Can I see your licence?"
5. The young man asked the girl, "Do you come here often?"
6. The tourists asked anxiously, "Is the castle haunted?"
7. The boy scout asked, "Do you want to cross the road?"
8. The newsagent asked me, "Do you want the papers cancelled?"
9. The manager asked me politely, "Do you wish to complain?"
10. The interviewer asked me, "Do you believe in the Loch Ness Monster?"

EXERCISE 3 (page 122)

1. When he hit himself with the hammer my father yelled, "Ouch!"
2. The enraged bus driver shouted, "Get out of the way!"
3. The mad professor whispered, "This will make you big and strong!"
4. The football supporters chanted, "Off!"
5. It came as quite a shock when Cynthia cried "Get lost!"
6. The bell rang and the referee shouted, "Seconds out!"
7. My friend Charlie frowned as I exclaimed, "Checkmate!"
8. All he could think of saying as the medal was placed around his neck was, "Ta!"
9. The ice opened up beneath them and I heard them cry, "Help!"
10. The audience applauded and cried, "Hear! Hear!"

EXERCISE 5 (page 124)

1. The doctor studied the X-ray plates carefully and said, "I've got some very good news for you."
2. I felt very flattered when some kids came up and asked, "Can we have your autograph?"
3. The chairman picked me out of the audience and asked, "What is your question?"
4. The whole town cheered as the Lone Ranger rode off into the sunset crying, "Hi-ho, Silver!"
5. The receptionist ran her finger down the page and asked sweetly, "What is your name again?"
6. Whenever things are going really badly I say to myself, "Worse things happen at sea."

Unit 2

Unit Test (page 125)

1. "I think you have dialled the wrong number," replied the operator.
2. "Hooray!" yelled the excited youngsters.
3. "Where is your absence note?" asked the teacher.
4. "Tell me all about it," said my granny.
5. "How many times do I have to tell you?" mumbled the prisoner.
6. "What a load of rubbish!" echoed round the stadium.

EXERCISE 1 (page 125)

1. "At last I will have a home of my own," he thought.
2. "I have been off work for the last two weeks," said my friend.
3. "You will have to make another appointment," explained the nurse.
4. "I have nothing to say at this point," muttered the Prime Minister.
5. "Whatever you do, don't panic," I said to myself.
6. "Grass doesn't grow on a busy street," answered my bald cousin.
7. "I think I've lost my pension book," sobbed the old lady.
8. "You will have to produce your passport," explained the travel agent.

EXERCISE 2 (page 126)

1. "What on earth do you mean?" asked Mr Jones.
2. "Can I go out and play?" asked Tommy.
3. "Could I have my bill now?" said the American tourist.
4. "Where did you go after the match?" asked his mother.
5. "Can I leave the table now?" asked his daughter.
6. "Where does it hurt?" inquired the doctor.
7. "When would you like to leave the island?" continued our host.
8. "Could you open your mouth a little wider, please?" whispered my dentist.

EXERCISE 3 (page 127)

1. "Look out!" yelled his father.
2. "Hands up!" snarled the bandit.
3. "Read all about it!" shouted the news-boy.
4. "Stand and deliver!" cried Dick Turpin.
5. "I submit!" moaned his opponent.
6. "Cut out the rough stuff!" ordered the referee.
7. "But I didn't take his wallet!" insisted Billy.
8. "Turn that radio off!" yelled my neighbour.

EXERCISE 4 (page 127)

1. "You have been found guilty of a very serious crime. I sentence you to five years imprisonment," said the judge.
2. "I am really sorry. I don't know what came over me." said the prisoner.
3. "I am becoming quite deaf. Speak up a bit," roared my uncle.
4. "Your father was a good man. We shall not see his like again," said Mr Brown sadly.
5. "That's all I can tell you at the moment. I hope to give you further information in the morning," said the captain.
6. "You can stop worrying now. We've landed safely," said the pilot's calm voice.

Unit 3

Unit Test (page 128)

1. "I will not go," he said, "for you or anyone."
2. "I don't really care," he replied, "one way or the other."
3. "But tell me," she asked, "what is the real reason?"
4. "If you don't wrap up warmly," said Alena, "you'll freeze."
5. "I don't wish to know that," I replied, "so kindly leave the stage."
6. "If at first you don't succeed," said the spider, "try, try, try again."

EXERCISE 1 (page 129)

1. If you are going to the shops," she asked, "will you buy me some fruit gums?"
2. "Despite my appalling rudeness," he pleaded, "can you find it in your heart to forgive me?"
3. "Stay in bed for a couple of days," ordered my doctor, "unless you want to catch pneumonia!"
4. "Hard to port," yelled the skipper, "or we'll hit the iceberg!"
5. "If you want to reach Bristol tonight," explained the porter, "you'll have to change at Crewe."
6. "If you promise not to tell a soul," whispered Agatha, "I'll let you into a little secret."

EXERCISE 2 (page 130)

1. "Thank you for all your help," said my neighbour. "I'll try to repay it some day."
2. "Do exactly as I say," whispered the sinister stranger. "You'll just have to trust me."
3. "I don't believe it," repeated the taxidermist. "I simply don't believe it."
4. "Could you give me a lift to London?" asked the red-faced man. "I will pay you well."
5. "Don't just stand there!" yelled my father. "Come into the house at once!"

Spelling List

This list is given here for easy reference and further spelling work. It includes all the words practised in the spelling modules on pages 29–76.

A

aboard
absence
accident
accommodation
account
accumulation
ache
achieve /-d
achievement
acquaintance
acquainted
acquired
action
addition
address
adopted
advantage
advantageous
adventure
advertisement
advice
afford
afterwards
again
agreed
agreement
agriculture
aircraft
aloud
already
although
altogether
always
amount
amusement
ancient
ankle
another
anxious
appearance
apple
appreciate
arguing
argument
arithmetic
article
assembly
association
attention
attractive
audience
August
aunt
awful

B

baffle
bakery
balance
balloon
bandage
barrel
barrier
beautiful
beautifully
beauty
because
beginning
behaviour
believe
believed
beneath
beneficial
benefited
benefiting
bible
blanket
blossom
blue
bomb
borrow
bottle
bought
boundaries
boundary
bowl
bread
breakfast
breast
breath
breathe
bright
brought
bubble
bucket
build
building
built
bulb
bundle
burial
buried
busily
business
busy
butcher
butterflies
butterfly
button

C

cabbage
calendar
calf
camera
candle
careful
carriage
carried
carrying
castle
catch
caught
cause
ceiling
celebrate
celery
central
centuries
century
certain
chain
chalk
change
changeable
character
cheerful
cheerfully
cherries
cherry
chicken
chief
children
chimney
chocolate
Christmas
church
circle
cities
city
clerk
climb
collection
colour
coloured
comb
comfortable
commerce
committee

communities
community
conceited
conceived
condition
conscience
conscious
cough
council
courage
courageous
court
cousin
crack
crawl
crept
cricket
crowd
crown
cruel
cruelly
crumb
curious
curtain
cushion

D

daily
damage
dance
dangerous
dangerously
daughter
death
deceive
deceived
December
defiance
defied
definite
definitely

definition
defying
degree
delicious
deliciously
delight
delighted
described
description
design
development
diamond
dictionaries
dictionary
difference
different
difficult
dinner
disappear
disappointment
disaster
disastrous
discover
disease
dissatisfied
distance
ditch
double
downstairs
drawn
drop
dropped
drown
drunk
due
duly
duties
duty
dwarf

E

each
eagle
earn
easier
easily
eastern
easy
edge
eight
eighth
eighty
either
electricity
embarrassed
embroidery
empty
enemy
energy
engine
engineer
enormous
enough
entertainment
entirely
envelope
environment
equal
equalled
equipment
escape
escaped
especially
Europe
everyone
everywhere
exactly
exaggerate
examination
example
excellent
excitable

excited
excitement
exciting
exercise
existence
expensive
experience
explain
express
extremely

F

factory
fairly
fairy
fame
families
family
famous
fascinated
fascination
father
favourite
feather
February
field
fierce
fiercely
finally
flour
flower
flying
forcible
foreign
forgotten
fought
found
four
fourth
freeze
freight

friend
friendship
fright
fruit
fuel
further

G

garage
gather
generally
gentle
gentleman
gently
geography
girl
going
government
graceful
gracefully
gradually
grease
green
groceries
growl
growth
guess
guidance
guide

H

handkerchief
happen
happened
happening
happiness
happy
harbour
hatch

haunt
hawk
headmaster
health
healthy
height
highway
history
hobby
honour
horrible
horribly
horse
hotel
house
household
however
husband

I

iceberg
imagine
immediately
importance
impossible
impossibly
improve
improvement
including
increase
independence
industries
industry
information
instance
instead
intelligence
interest
invention
invitation
irrigation

irritated

J

jacket
January
jealous
jewel
jewellery
journal
judge
juice
July
jump
June
jungle
junior
justice

K

kettle
kingdom
kitchen
knee
knelt
knew
knife
knight
knitting
knock
know
knowledge
knowledgeable

L

labour
lamb
lamp

language
laugh
laughable
laughed
laughter
lawyer
league
least
leather
leisure
length
letter
lettuce
liberty
libraries
library
lightening
likelihood
limb
liquid
lorries
lorry
lovable
lung

M

machinery
magazine
majority
manufacture
marble
march
March
marriage
married
marry
match
meanwhile
measles
measure
medicine

member
memories
memory
merciless
mercy
method
midnight
mighty
military
milk
minute
mischief
mischievous
modelled
moisture
money
morning
mother
mountain
mouse
movable
multiply
mysterious
mystery

N

naughty
necessary
needle
neighbour
neither
nephew
newspaper
next
night
noisily
northern
nothing
notice
noticeable
November

nuisance
number
numerous
nylon

O

oasis
occasion
occupation
occur
occurred
occurrence
October
officer
once
onion
operation
opportunity
opposite
orange
orchard
orchestra
owner
oxygen
oyster

P

paddle
palace
palm
paragraph
parliament
peace
peaceable
peaceful
pencilled
penguin
people
perceive

perceived
permission
photograph
phrase
piano
picked
picture
piece
pigeon
playing
pleasurable
pleasure
plough
poison
possession
possible
powder
practice
practise
preferred
primary
principal
principle
probable
probably
problem
proceed
programme
proud
puncture
pursue
puzzle
pyjamas

Q

qualities
quality
quantities
quantity
question
queue

quickly
quiet
quietly

R

rabbit
read
really
receive
received
recommended
recreation
refer
referee
referred
referring
regret
regrettable
relieved
religious
remember
rescue
rhythm
rough
round
rugby

S

saddle
safety
sailor
salmon
sandwich
saucepan
saucer
sausage
scarce
scarf
scene

scenery
school
science
scratch
secondary
secretary
seize
sentence
separate
separated
separately
September
settlement
seventh
shadow
shelves
shoe
shopping
should
shoulder
sight
similar
sincere
sincerely
single
skipping
slippery
smoking
soccer
somewhere
soup
special
specially
splendid
square
stable
starch
stationary
stationery
statue
stomach
straight
stranger

street
strength
student
studied
studying
subject
subtraction
succeed
success
successful
successfully
suddenly
suggest
suit
surprised
surround
swim
swimming
swing
system

T

table
target
taught
tease
teaspoon
telegraph
temperature
tennis
terrible
terrified
terrifying
thankful
theatre
their
there
therefore
thief
think
third
thirsty

thought
thoughtful
thousand
thread
three
through
ticket
tight
toe
tobacco
tomatoes
tongue
tough
traffic
train
transferred
traveller
treasure
tried
trouble
trousers
true
truly
turtle
twice
twins
typewriter

U

ugly
umbrella
umpire
underneath
unknown
unless
unnecessary
useful

V

valuable
value
variety
view
vinegar
violin
voice

W

waist
walk
waste
wealthy
weather
weave
weight
weird
western
whatever
wheat
whenever
where
whether
which
while
whip
whispered
whistle
white
who
whole
whose
width
window
witch
wolf
wolves
wonderful
worthy
would
wound
wrist
write
writing
wrong

Y

year
yield